RELATIONAL GENIUS

RELATIONAL GENIUS

The High Achiever's Guide
to Soft-Skill Confidence
in Leadership and Life

TRICIA S. GROFF, PhD

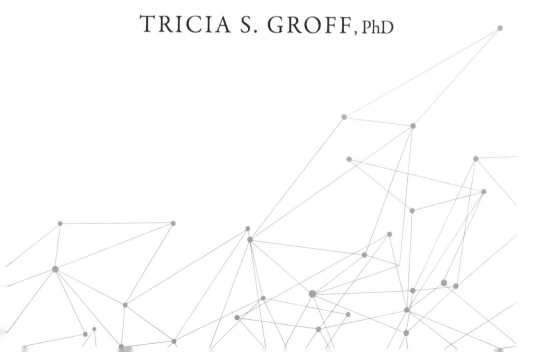

*To Dr. Al Forsyth, who taught me
that I didn't have to choose between
being smart and having fun.*

CONTENTS

PART II. GETTING PEOPLE TO TAKE YOU SERIOUSLY

PART III. UNDERSTANDING AND ASSESSING OTHER PEOPLE

PART IV. TOXIC GAMES: THE DIFFICULT PEOPLE PLAYBOOK

PART V. HOW DO I SAY THAT?

WARNING:
YOU'RE GOING TO HATE THIS

"You're going to hate this." My client sighed and rolled his eyes. He is a high achiever who likes action plans, as long as those plans don't involve emotions. I proceeded to outline my recommendations to address the human variables present in the situation.

"That's going to be uncomfortable," he said.

"And?" I shrugged. "You want to be excellent, right? You're not paying me to tell you what's easy."

I am an executive coach for high achievers, and I routinely tell them things they hate. If you are a high achiever, especially an analytical one, I wrote this book for you. You will likely hate some of it. You might not want to deal with emotions and people, or you feel like you should already know the information.

I know your time is valuable, so I want to set appropriate expectations up front. While I believe you will benefit from staying the course through any discomfort, I also want to be honest about what the book is and what it is not.

This book is for you if:

a. You want practical information to help you understand and navigate people.

b. You want specific tactics and game plans, especially for Difficult People.

c. You are open-minded, love learning, and are willing to think outside of the box.

d. You don't actually read whole books, but you want to reference helpful sections.

e. You like books that say many things instead of the same thing over and over again.

It's not for you if:

a. You want an academic read. While I am trained in research, this practical guide is long on tactics and short on theory.

b. You value convention. I fuse incongruous concepts to focus on "what works." You may find unusual suggestions or a spiritual reference and a swear word in the same chapter.

Do you need to be a high achiever to gain value from the book? No. I believe many topics discussed—like knowing whom to trust—can help anyone. At the same time, I write as if I am speaking to one of my clients, and so you will notice the high achiever assumption.

How do you know if you are a high achiever? If you are a high achiever, you have high expectations. You believe you should be competent, kind, and effective in all situations. You take responsibility seriously, and you believe other people should do the same. You strive to interact with honesty and integrity, and you are dumbfounded when others don't. Incompetence in other people makes you want to scream, and incompetence in yourself makes you want to hide. Everyone views you as successful, but on the inside you sometimes ask, "Am I enough?" or "Am I handing this the right way?" You are performance-oriented. If you're an analytical high achiever, situations that require high emotional output exhaust you. You want to get along with people, but sometimes people wear you out. If you're still reading, this book is probably for you.

I arrived at the critical information in this book through experience. I obtained my bachelor's, master's, and doctorate degrees in psychology, with honors at each level; yet I came to fully understand the complexity of relationships through working with my clients and my own pursuit of interpersonal excellence. Although the information I present is based on psychological principles, it focuses on gritty application. I will give you answers for the most common question, asked with a wealth of frustration: *"But, Tricia, what do I do?"*

In the following pages, I'm going to walk you through the fundamentals of understanding yourself and your own emotions, interacting effectively with others, responding appropriately to Difficult People, and knowing what to say in sticky situations. I've included specific content for those of you who are leaders.

None of us learn human behavior in one sitting, and all high achievers are action-oriented. Thus, the layout of this book allows you to quickly reference topics and the associated recommendations. Included throughout the book are the following:

1. Lists of tactics to make abstract ideas concrete and actionable

2. Quotes from other high achievers to remind you that you are not alone

3. Leadership Application boxes to guide those of you in positions of leadership

4. Specific scripts to answer the question "How do I say that?"

5. Links to the *www.relationalgenius.com* resource site to help you master specific challenges

Sometimes I even tell you when you can skip or skim sections and refer back to them later through the detailed table of contents at the beginning of the book.

At this point, you might still be left with this question: *Why should I read a book I might hate?*

I could tell you about some clients' success stories. I could tell you about the gains you will make in your personal and professional life. I could probably shame you for leaving the complexity of human behavior unchallenged. Instead, I am going to tell you that effectively navigating yourself and others brings confidence and freedom.

As we grow more confident in ourselves and our decision-making about people, we free ourselves. We free ourselves from energy drains, emotional clutter, self-doubt, bad business partnerships, and time-sucks. We free ourselves to invest in positive relationships instead of trying to fix the broken ones. And out of this freedom, we buy our lives back. We increase our excellence. We achieve more peace. We have more fun. Ready? I believe in you. You've got this.

Successful Sam

Why is this so hard? I feel like I'm missing a skillset that is fundamentally human.

Logical Larry

Tricia, I have such a hard time ego-stroking at work. I'm honest, and I don't play games. Some people don't understand that. Is something wrong with me?

Caring Carrie

Tricia, I trust people. Now I feel naive for taking them at their word.

Part I

—

YOU

Chapter 1

HIGH ACHIEVERS AND SOFT-SKILLS DEVELOPMENT

I was role-playing with one of my smartest clients. In this case, his cognitive intelligence didn't solve the problem. I was teaching him emotional intelligence. He was walking into a high-stakes situation, and I needed him to present as a formidable opponent. "Okay, I need you to intimidate me," I told him. He puffed up his shoulders like a confused eagle. I laughed and showed him how to rearrange his facial expression to project power.

A lot of high achievers feel a discrepancy between their cognitive prowess and their soft skills. Before we go into mending this disparity, let me delineate the high achiever reference. There is no formal "high achiever" classification, and many smart people may not fit my high achiever profile. So how do you know if I'm talking to you?

I operationally define a "high achiever" according to an amalgamation of personality characteristics. While many people in leadership positions are high achievers, the term does not refer to status or professional success.

Below is a list of common high achiever characteristics. High achievers have different patterns, so you may identify with many but not all of these traits.

1. People tell you that you have high expectations, but your expectations make perfect sense to you.

2. You feel responsible for the outcomes of situations, even if you are only part of the equation, and even if some factors are outside of your control.

3. You are innately honest.

4. You hate incompetence.

5. You feel embarrassed or ashamed when you make mistakes.

6. People give you high praise, but you often feel deficient.

7. You have a contradiction inside of yourself. You objectively know you perform better than most people, but you simultaneously wonder if you are "good enough."

8. You're a big-picture thinker, and tedium makes you cry.

9. You're open-minded, and you love learning.

10. You hate drama and highly nuanced social interactions.

11. You felt different from other kids when you were growing up.

12. You hate disappointing people.

13. You dislike small talk.

14. It's hard for you to ask for help.

15. Emotions stress you out.

16. You use logical arguments to solve emotional problems.
    (It doesn't work.)

17. You struggle with work-life balance.

18. You skip book introductions. (I specifically didn't call mine
    "Introduction" because I knew you'd skip it. If you skipped
    it anyway, go back and read "*Warning*: You're Going to
    Hate This.")

I have a condensed list of those characteristics on my website,
and the contrasting reactions amuse me. One man called me and

said, "Yes, that's me! It's like you met me." A woman confessed, "I was a little embarrassed to find I had several of the qualities on your list." Someone else told me she was going to hire a low-level coach until she could be good enough to work with me.

All of those reactions reflect a perception about whether being a high achiever is bad or good. I simply view it as a personality style that is not intrinsically either. Sometimes, my clients will ask me if their thought processes are normal. My reaction is usually "Not compared to everyone else, but this is typical for high achievers."

High achievers usually want to keep all of the positive characteristics of their personality style and omit the problematic ones. I'm on board with the intention, but it doesn't work that way. A lot of traits act as a strength in one situation but as a detriment, or shadow side, in another. My strength, as a high achiever, is that I want to give my best to people; the shadow side of that characteristic is that I may overwork because I don't have an accurate gauge of what is good enough.

For many high achievers, lower soft-skills development is the shadow side of early intellectual focus. If you are like my high-achieving clients, you are more comfortable in your cognitive acumen than in your soft skills. You care about people, but people drive you crazy. Hence, we will start with the themes I have noticed in high achievers' soft-skills development. Some of the information may not fit you. That's normal. I am purposefully generalizing for efficiency, but not all high achievers are created equal. Take what applies to you, and leave the rest.

© Dr. Tricia Groff

SOFT-SKILLS DEVELOPMENT IN HIGH ACHIEVERS

It's natural to assume that we should understand people. If we are *homo sapiens*, shouldn't we have the inside knowledge to excel in all things human? On the contrary, the study of human behavior is fraught with contradictions and inaccurate metrics. The most rigorous psychological studies are unlikely to produce cause-and-effect relationships. If psychologists have a hard time understanding humans, where does that leave you?

It's important to realize that you are not unique in your occasional (or frequent) confusion about navigating people. If you believe you have an intrinsic deficit and beat yourself up about it, you'll avoid the learning process. In fact, the first step to building relational confidence is to accept that the learning curve is normal.

You may be saying, "But, Tricia, I *know* other people are better at soft skills than I am." That may be true, but your assumption that others automatically "get it" is not. Many people, whom others view as successful and confident, prepare extensively to have a specific conversation. Sometimes I help clients do awkward, painstaking role-plays to prepare for a presentation. The only thing their colleagues see is a polished professional who feels confident and at ease. What looks "natural" took a lot of practice.

People ask me if soft skills are innate or learned. The answer is "both." As children, we invest in the activities that we are naturally good at or affirmed for doing. If we struggle academically, we may pursue sports. If social interactions are challenging, we may focus on intellectual success.

Many high achievers received early validation for performance. If this recognition occurred when we were otherwise rejected by peers or parents, the validation became powerful because we felt accepted. Praise is an excellent substitute for unconditional love. We remember the praise and protect our self-worth by focusing on achievement as a substitute for belonging. Our focus on achievement can decrease the frequency of our social interactions, thus slowing our soft-skills development.

Parents and teachers also influence our soft-skills development. As children, we assume that adult behavior is a template for what is normal. We learn implicitly from their actions, subconsciously developing emotional and social rules based on what we see. If we are fortunate, an adult may explain how to optimize soft skills, but even this explicit instruction originates from their own biases about how to navigate relationships. Frequently, we are left with few clear instructions and an array of contradictory conclusions that confound the most socially competent among us.

We believe that other people deserve second chances, but we need to draw lines on how many chances we give. We want to go the extra mile to serve others, but we don't want to be a doormat. We want to trust people, but people have burned us. We want to be excellent, but sometimes our expectations of ourselves hurt us. How do we reconcile all of the inconsistencies? We don't. We use the tension in the dance to make intelligent decisions about humanity without losing heart.

As you move forward in this process, remember: **you will always be in the learning curve when it comes to understanding yourself and others.** The confusing and paradoxical implications of human behavior can frustrate all of us. The good news is that there are fundamental concepts that allow us to navigate the social matrix more easily.

In the next chapter, we start with the critical foundation of soft-skills acquisition—understanding yourself. Self-knowledge, especially about your idiosyncrasies, will enhance your interactions with others. This understanding will also inform the way you integrate all other suggestions in this book.

KEY TAKEAWAYS

1. *Many high achievers lack confidence in their soft skills. You are not alone.*

2. *Early validation for performance coupled with interpersonal rejection may inhibit soft-skills development.*

3. *You will always be in the learning curve about human behavior.*

Chapter 2

WHO ARE YOU AND HOW DO PEOPLE SEE YOU?

"How has it taken me 40 years to learn this about myself?"
—From a CIO who specializes in
complex problem-solving

Have you ever tried to figure out if someone was avoiding you or was merely bad at communicating? Or maybe you've had a cranky colleague, and you are never sure if he is grumpy at the world or specifically toward you? By contrast, don't you love when someone tells you she hates mornings and her lack of engagement isn't personal?

Our behavior makes sense to us, so we assume that other people understand it as well. They don't. If you are quiet and a little shy, some people will perceive you as introverted; others will view you as aloof or judgmental. One of my clients is intense and direct; others perceive him as angry.

The first step to improving soft skills is knowing your patterns. Since you are the variable over which you have the most control in any human interaction, understanding yourself will optimize all interpersonal strategies you can use. When we are aware of our idiosyncrasies, we can teach people how to interpret our actions. This knowledge helps them to feel comfortable with us.

I know, for example, that I am emotionally unavailable when I am focused. It's a personality quirk—part of who I am. If someone meets me when I am relaxed, they perceive me as bubbly, easygoing, and kind. When I am focused, I am intense and minimally responsive. The shift makes people feel that I'm angry, tense, or disengaged. Hence, I use this script when I meet people who will regularly interact with me.

> **Script:** "Just to give you a heads-up, I tend to be much less talkative or engaged when I'm focused. It's not that I'm angry or trying to be dismissive."

If I share this at the front end of our engagement, I create little categories in their heads for "Tricia-available" versus "Tricia-focused." This knowledge allows them to read my behavior and lowers the chances of hurt feelings.

The more you own your idiosyncrasies, the better you can explain them to others. If you view your peculiarities as weaknesses, you won't use this tactic. You will worry about creating an unfavorable first impression by mentioning them. This rationale is problematic because people notice our behavior and make assumptions, whether we want them to or not. When we initiate the conversation, we tell them how to read us and what conclusions to draw.

We don't need to apologize for ourselves when we own our idiosyncrasies. People don't have a problem with imperfection; they do have a problem with ambiguous cues that leave them confused about our intentions. People feel safe when they know what to expect, and telling them what to expect automatically enhances the relationship.

You need to know a little bit about yourself to tell people how to read you. Additionally, when you understand yourself, you will have more control over the one variable (you) that is present in all interpersonal conundrums. So what do you know about yourself? Below are some self-knowledge questions and common high achiever responses.

SELF-KNOWLEDGE QUESTIONS

What frustrates you?
"Incompetence. It drives me crazy. I'm more likely to be a jerk when I encounter it, and sometimes I'm sarcastic about it."

What brings out your best?
"When I feel simultaneously appreciated and challenged."

What brings out your worst?
"Micromanagement. Emotional fatigue. Working hard with no measurable results. Interpersonal drama or friction."

What are your dominant personality features?
"Direct, analytical, ambitious, responsible, caring."

How are you most likely to be misunderstood?
"Sometimes, my directness is taken as rudeness. Or I'm ana-
lyzing a problem, and I inadvertently hurt someone's feelings.
I use dry humor, and sometimes it offends people."

What's your leadership style?
"I try to be steady and even-handed, but I get frustrated when
people don't follow through on simple tasks. I know I need
to delegate, but sometimes it feels better to do it myself."

Using the self-knowledge questions above as a starting point, figure
out which of your personality characteristics might confuse others.
You may want to ask a trusted colleague or a friend for feedback.
(You can download self-knowledge questionnaires at *www.relational
genius.com*.)

Difficult People Warning: Be sure to read Part IV of
this book before disclosing your idiosyncrasies to
unknown others. Unstable or untrustworthy people
will try to use them against you.

In the next chapter, you will find essential self-knowledge components to help you master emotion. When we identify and cope
with feelings, we optimize all other soft skills.

KEY TAKEAWAYS

1. *The better you understand yourself and your responses to situations, the better you can help other people understand you.*

2. *If you don't explain an idiosyncrasy, you leave space for others to make inaccurate assumptions. Not sharing who you are may save your ego, but you limit your interpersonal effectiveness.*

3. *Don't apologize for your needs or quirks. Simply understand them for yourself first, then explain them to those in your surroundings.*

LEADERSHIP APPLICATION

Building Trust with Teams

As a leader, you don't want your team to have to figure out who you are. When you help them understand your leadership style, stress points, and expectations, it builds trust. Team culture flows from the leader, so the techniques you use to develop trust with your subordinates provide a model of how they can build trust with each other.

Business Partnerships, Investors, New Leadership

Whether you are hammering out a business partnership, getting investors on board, or leading a new company, you want to explain who you are and how people should read you. Essentially, when the stakes are high for you and the other person/entity, you want to come across as a steady and trustworthy leader. No one is perfect, but showing self-awareness goes a long way.

Chapter 3

EMOTIONS—I KNOW YOU WANT TO SKIP THEM

Special reminder for this chapter. In the section on specific emotions, you may want to jump to the emotions that are most relevant for you now, and skip or skim the rest until you need it. You'll be able to use the table of contents to refer back to a specific emotion whenever you need the information.

"Dr. Tricia, can you help me feel the positive emotions but not the negative ones?"

—From a healthcare executive

walked out of the grocery store not seeing the people around me. I was lost in thought. *How do I convince people to read about emotions?* I wondered. *Emotional competence is critical to performance and leadership, but my clients hate emotion. Wait, why do high achievers hate negative emotions so much?* An answer popped into my head. *Because negative emotions feel bad. No one likes to experience stuff that makes them feel bad.* Brilliant deduction, but was it this simple?

Unsatisfied with my answer, I texted some of my clients: *Favor, can you tell me why you dislike your own negative emotions? The first thing that pops into your head.* Below are some answers I received:

"It feels bad. Physically feels bad."

"I was taught to buck up and not wallow in them. If I feel them, I think I'm weak or doing something wrong."

"Ugh. It just sits there and is super uncomfortable. It's hard to get out the negative feelings without a lot of effort."

"I grew up with negative emotion, and it became part of me. I've worked so hard to limit those emotions, and I beat myself up when I let them take over the positive emotions."

"I'm not productive when I spend time on them. When the emotion recedes, I regret the wasted time."

"They bring me down. They're exhausting."

After reading the texts, I realized something. I still hate negative emotions. I default to happy, and I like to be productive. Dealing with negative emotions is tiring. So why do I want you to deal with them? Let me give you my personal answer first.

Coping with negative emotion helps me to feel at peace and in control, even when I am upset. I don't like the feelings or the energy required to navigate them, but I know what is happening. This awareness helps me to be present and effective. I feel power because I know my emotional reactions are not facts. Thus, they don't scare or overwhelm me. Emotional competence also increases my effectiveness, my relationship skills, and my decision-making.

Emotional competence increases our effectiveness because we can run clean. Years ago, a 12-year-old client asked me the purpose of dealing with negative emotions. "Tricia, why do we have to do this? Bad stuff happened. Talking about it makes me feel sad. What's the point?" It was a great question, so I asked my supervisor. He said, "When we have a glass of water with dirt in it, and we pour clean water on top of it, the dirt infects the clean water, no matter how much we pour on top." Dealing with negative emotions gets the dirt out. You can let them move through you and out of you, so you can move forward.

Emotional competence also increases our relationship skills. Comfort with the discomfort of negative emotion helps us empathize with other people's feelings. When you understand and respond to others' emotions, you help them to trust you. If you are like most high achievers, you will pretend you can be effective with other people's feelings, even if you can't deal with your own. Unfortunately, it doesn't work that way. Emotions aren't a textbook that you can read and then decide to differentially apply knowledge wherever you want.

Finally, emotional competence enhances decision-making. In one of my past professional lives, I specialized in traumatic brain injury. People who had brain damage such that they felt no emotion struggled to make decisions. Our emotions cut through the logical morass of information overload, guide decision-making, and foster insight. You've heard of the term "gut feelings." Sometimes our brain synthesizes information faster than we can logically process an answer. Our brain's nervous system connects to the second nervous system in our gut, called the enteric nervous system. Our tummies may hurt, signaling a threat or a conclusion about a situation before we fully comprehend the facts at hand. **Hence, using emotion as a source of information increases our efficiency.**

If you can figure out why you want to get better with emotion, you will be more likely to apply the strategies and tactics that follow.

I promise you two things as we move forward:

1. I will not ask you to marinate in negative emotion.

2. I will give you tools to help you feel in control of emotion.

WHY ARE EMOTIONS HARD FOR HIGH ACHIEVERS?

Many high achievers push away emotions because they had to raise themselves emotionally. If your parents were emotional train wrecks or dismissive of emotion, you learned to cope with your feelings independently. You probably pushed them away because there were no adults to comfort you. Maybe you were in a household where you were taking care of everyone else's emotions, and there simply wasn't space for your own. Some of my clients learned early to only rely on themselves. If you have no one to lean on, negative emotion becomes a liability because you need all of your resources to survive.

Maybe you had emotionally supportive parents, but you still hate negative emotions. Why? Emotions make us feel incompetent, powerless, and tired. Our intellect, on the other hand, allows us to be precise and in control. Thus, we intellectualize emotion instead of feeling it.

As a high achiever who struggles with negative emotions, you likely think they are wrong or make you weak. Please trust me on this—negative emotions are not related to strength or intelligence. Unless you have extensive brain damage, you will feel all emotions, so let's learn what to do with them.

Today 12:03 PM

Ugh why is this so hard and so sad. I just need to work through these feelings which I just have to let run their course and accept myself as human and with that i will become attached to people and care about them. And that really just makes me normal I guess but ugh feelings suck

Text Message

We often want to put negative emotions into a tidy box, up on a shelf, where they can't hurt us. The problem with that strategy is that the box will fall off the shelf at the most inopportune time, raining emotions down on our heads. If we keep using the following responses, we fail with emotion:

1. "It's in the past, and there is nothing I can do to change it. No point in getting upset about it."

2. "Well, I made the wrong choice, so it's my fault. I shouldn't be upset about it."

3. "I shouldn't let it bother me."

When we experience feelings and make peace with them, we lower the chances that we will have boxes of negative emotions stuck inside of our brains. We gain power because we can control the feelings instead of allowing them to subconsciously drive us. Below, I will give you specific tactics on how to handle negative emotions. Familiarizing yourself with the coping strategies takes a little practice. Be patient with yourself.

Note: The explanations and strategies for the emotions below do not account for common mental health concerns such as depression, generalized anxiety, or other mood-related problems. If it feels like the emotions or lack thereof cause you significant distress or interfere with daily functioning, see a mental health professional to help you sort through them. Please be aware that many people could be legitimately diagnosed with a mental health concern at some point in life. It's often a combination of genetic and situational factors. It's not a characterological flaw.

SADNESS AND GRIEF

"I have a company to run. People depend on me."

"I'm the only person in the family who has her stuff together. I can't afford to lose it."

"I don't have time to be sad."

Do any of these sound like you? When you're in a leadership position, the sadness itself is compounded by the fear of falling apart and not handling your obligations. The standard advice of "Let it all out" is scary for high achievers and probably many other people. High achievers ask, "What if I let it out and lose control? What if I can't put it back in the box?" Here's the thing: **if we stuff sadness down, we lose control anyway.**

If you don't let the sadness move through you, it will

1.   bite you in the butt when it is least convenient; and

2.   make you physically sick.

Emotionally traumatic experiences affect us at a neurological level, setting new defaults without our conscious permission. The change is subtle—motivation gradually decreases as we also begin to experience body aches, weight gain, and less enjoyment of daily life. Ten years later, we realize that our tidy package of emotion has controlled us. We have two choices regarding sadness and grief: deal with it now when it hasn't affected so many layers of our lives, or deal with it later when it is unmanageable and inconvenient. Some high achievers internalize emotions, and their bodies—rather than their hearts—tell the story.

Physical Signs of Grief

Analytical people do not always know that they are sad, and their body has to tell them—through headaches, interrupted sleep, lethargy, and indigestion. A few months after my father died, I noticed periodic numbness in my feet. I was a little concerned, so I began tracking the occurrences on a calendar. During that period, I heard someone make an offhanded comment: "You know how your body sometimes goes a little numb during grief?" I didn't know. I tuned into myself and realized that I was sadder than I thought. I sorted through the emotion, and I never had the numbness again.

Common Physical Symptoms of Grief
- Headaches
- Lack of energy
- Indigestion or appetite changes
- Body aches
- Dizziness
- Increased inflammatory markers
- Heartache (literal)
- Cognitive Signs of Grief

"My brain feels like a sieve. I forget a lot of things," my client said. This is another common statement people make after experiencing grief and loss. High stress impacts memory. Stress makes us distractible, and distraction reduces our ability to encode information into memory. During these times, we can feel like we are "losing our mind." We forget things quickly or lose our thoughts in the middle of sentences. This symptom is short-term and will recede as we heal. Compensate by writing everything down so that you minimize the stress of relying on your short-term memory.

Common Cognitive Symptoms of Grief

- Distractibility
- Difficulty concentrating
- Short-term memory loss
- Mental fog
- Increased difficulty staying on track in conversations
- "Spacing out" and forgetting what you are supposed to be doing

What to Expect about the Course of Grief

Grief responses don't follow the neat little patterns you see on some websites. You might be angry, annoyed, relieved, or happy at any point in time. If you've experienced an extreme loss, expect grief to come in waves and hit when you are least expecting it. That pattern can be frustrating because you'll think that you are feeling better and then get caught off guard with a bad day. Over time, the waves will be less frequent or less intense.

Try not to worry about dealing with it "the right way." You may be worried about lowering your productivity or letting the grief get out of hand. One of my friends was concerned that he would use grief as an excuse for laziness. These concerns are common for high achievers.

The only way you can mess up the grief process is to ignore it and pretend that you're okay. You can also increase your misery by pressuring yourself to maintain the same high level of performance. It's better to assume that your performance will be compromised and build the margins to accommodate the deficit.

Remember to give yourself permission to grieve losses that are not death. Loss of dreams, loss of professional or personal identity, loss of relationships—all of these incur grief. It's easy to downplay loss with statements such as "It could be worse. I don't have it that bad. I shouldn't feel this sad." Those thought processes minimize normal, healthy emotional responses.

Finally, remember that sadness and grief are signs of living well. We cannot hope, risk, love, and live...without engaging loss. The only way to avoid sadness and grief is to stay on the sidelines and not live at all.

Suggestions to Help You Cope with Sadness and Grief

1. Ice cream (just kidding)

2. Crying boxes—this tactic helps high achievers feel in control. I use the term "boxes" because we are putting parameters on the amount of crying. We give ourselves permission to cry without worrying that it will take over the day. Set a timer—say, for 15 minutes—and allow

yourself to be sad. When the timer goes off, get up and move. You can use whatever time interval feels right to you. Implement the tactic when you feel a wave of sadness. Eventually, you'll feel more confident that you can experience your feelings without losing control.

3. Identify three people who will be supportive in the way that you need them to be. Support may be a hug, a beer, a listening ear, or a stupid joke.

4. Don't try to make yourself happy. Distance yourself from the people who minimize your emotion with comments like "It could be worse" or "There's a reason for everything."

5. Journal. Talk with a friend. Talk with a therapist. Or do all of these. Sadness and grief exist in layers. Examining their complexity allows us to gain insight and heal.

6. After you've allowed yourself time to grieve, try to find meaning. Is there something you can learn through the sadness? Don't try to get to the meaning-making stage too quickly; remember that you want to give yourself space to process the emotion first.

7. Look for places to be grateful. Do not minimize the sadness. Simply keep your eyes open for beautiful moments.

LEADERSHIP APPLICATION

Safeguards

If you are a business owner or a leader who manages a lot of detail, ask a trusted colleague or partner to help you not drop a ball. This strategy benefits both of you. It removes your burden of triple-checking everything due to distractibility or memory glitches. It also frees the other person to point out errors without worrying about offending you.

Give People the Basics and Tell Them How to Help

The degree to which you give details is entirely up to you. You can simply note that you have a difficult personal matter, or you can provide specific information. You can ask for privacy, flexibility, extra reminders...whatever will help you. A lot of people want to be helpful, but they don't know how. Tell people what might work best for you.

HURT

Full disclosure: After I wrote this section, I got my feelings hurt—badly. I, a licensed psychologist with 20 years of experience, lay in bed at 12:30 a.m., searching the web for "how to cope with hurt feelings." I knew the answers, but I needed someone else to walk me through them. As with grief, hurt feelings occur when we live fully.

We usually get hurt when we risk our hearts in some way, either professionally or personally. I can't tell you how to value relationships without getting your feelings hurt, but I will walk you through some coping strategies.

First, banish the term "oversensitive." I think the term was designed by people who can't handle emotions and make others feel guilty for having them. When taken literally, it's a ridiculous concept that leaves us asking, "How much sensitivity is enough?" If you are a high achiever, you do not have a victim mentality, and you do not think that everyone is personally attacking you. Hence, you are not "oversensitive." Your time is better used to analyze the hurt and walk through it.

Our feelings get hurt when we think that someone might not value us as highly as we value them. Sometimes our feelings get hurt when someone criticizes our performance. In our Western culture, we learn that we are not supposed to care about what other people think, but this idea is absurd. We all want to be valued; this desire is a fundamental part of being human.

While hurt feelings are normal, the conclusions we make based on hurt feelings may or may not be accurate. Have you every snapped at someone you loved because you were tired? Or made a snide comment at work because you were stressed? All of us have "off" days when we say or do things that don't reflect our actual value for the other person.

Unfortunately, knowing all of the above doesn't instantly make the hurt go away. We have expectations about how people should act if they like us. If their behavior does not match our expectations, we conclude that they do not value us as much as we thought they did. We feel weak and vulnerable, and we just want the pain to stop.

Questions and Tactics to Deal with Hurt

1. "Do I believe this person is intentionally trying to hurt me?" If your answer is yes, you need to rethink the relationship. If your answer is no, assess the other variables that may contribute to his or her actions.

2. In a close relationship, tell someone that your feelings got hurt. I try to take ownership to avoid blaming the other person for something that wasn't their intention.

Script: "I got my feelings hurt when _____ happened. I'm pretty sure that wasn't the intention. Can we figure out a different approach the next time?"

3. Does this person behave this way only with you or with other people as well?

4. Is your hurt specific to the situation at hand, or does it also remind you of historical wounds? Sometimes emotional traumatic events are not processed and stored properly in our brains. Thus, later similar experiences, however distantly linked, can trigger a strong response. If your reaction is intense, try to figure out how it connects to previous experiences. This strategy helps you objectively understand why the hurt is so intense.

5. Give yourself time to process hurt, and ask others to give you time. Sometimes we're hurt, but we don't understand why. We need time to explain it, even to ourselves.

6. If you have a close friend that you trust, call him or her and talk about it. High achievers tend to deal with hurt alone or numb it with substances. It takes guts to call a friend, but the reassurance helps.

Finally, it's important to recognize that we often get our feelings hurt when there is a mismatch of love languages (e.g., your fantastic present isn't appreciated because the other person doesn't care about gifts). Knowing how other people "love" protects feelings in both personal and professional relationships. For more information on love languages, check out *The 5 Love Languages* by Gary Chapman.

Apologize When You Have Hurt Others

A lot of high achievers have been hurt by those who repeatedly apologize without changing their behavior. Thus, it is easy to decide not to apologize because apologies "don't mean anything." The refusal to apologize creates a problem when the only action that the hurt person wants is an apology.

Omitting the apology makes you look weak. Others can see that you feel regretful but that you are unable or unwilling to apologize. An apology, coupled with congruent actions, is the fastest way to put a relationship back on track.

Additional Tactics for When You Hurt Others

1. If you hurt people's feelings, affirm their value. Follow up with actions—a card or a home-cooked meal. If the hurt is severe, add additional efforts that are spaced out over time. This sustained effort shows that you understand the hurt you created and reassures the other person of his or her value.

   Script: "I am so sorry that I forgot about our plans. I know it was hurtful, even if that wasn't my intention. Could we look at the calendar and figure out a different day to celebrate?"

2. Give the other person time. It is insulting to try to make someone feel okay as fast as possible to make your discomfort go away.

3. Apologize immediately. Waiting a few days when you know you've screwed up is stupid. It gives the other person a lot of time to think about the hurt and build all sorts of mental explanations about why you don't value them.

4. In professional settings, apologize in person and follow up with a note one week later. Handwritten notes remove the pressure to respond, and they show that you are serious about repairing the relationship.

Can you do email or text follow-ups? Yes, but tell the other person that you don't need a response. It's wrong to make a person you've hurt feel additional pressure to respond. A handwritten note or a card takes extra effort, and that is why I recommend it.

FEAR

What are you afraid of? Relationships? Maybe. Finances? Sometimes. What about failure, making wrong decisions, and public embarrassment? Now we're talking. Failure gets close to a core fear—that of not being "enough."

> *"Everyone thinks I'm amazing, but what if they get to know me and decide that they don't like me?"*
> —From many, many clients

I've tried to avoid redundancy in this book, but you'll see that the high achiever's concern about being "good enough" repeats itself from several angles. High achievers get a lot of accolades for performance, such that failure feels like death. As I mentioned earlier, we often conflate praise and love. Thus, if we get continued validation from our successes, an insidious question begins to form: "Am I still valuable if I mess up?"

If performance helps us feel that we belong, then failure in performance creates the fear of rejection. Most high achievers I know feel bad about themselves if they fail. Hence, failure becomes a double-edged sword. It has the potential to slice from within (disappointment in ourselves) and from without (rejection from others). Many surface-level stressors can be traced to subconscious fears of being "enough." Below are starting points to challenge that core concern.

"I want to read all of the books on leadership and work with you so that I don't make any mistakes."

—From a Fortune 100 leader

How to Deal with Fears of Failure and of Not Being "Enough"

1. Figure out when you first believed that you weren't "enough." Maybe someone overtly told you that you were deficient. Perhaps someone emotionally neglected you. Alternately, maybe you only got attention for achievements and deduced that those comprise your value.

2. Work through the fear with a coach or a therapist. Anxiety about being "enough" links to self-worth, and it's hard to figure it out alone.

3. Read chapter 5 on confidence and check out the in-depth study online at *www.relationalgenius.com.*

In addition to our deep personal fears, we encounter daily worries. Will a deal go through? Can I fire this person without a lawsuit? Will the kids be okay? My clients dislike the "f" word so much that I give them a standing ovation when they tell me they're afraid. If you believe that you should be strong, confident, and impervious to fear, you put extra stress on yourself.

Not only is fear normal, but it can help us identify risk. When the coronavirus hit in early 2020, I had one question for all of my business owners: "How much runway do you have?" I was scared with them, and looking at the best- and worst-case scenarios helped us make difficult decisions. So how do you use fear instead of allowing it to paralyze you?

How to Deal with Daily Fears

1. Gather the data to assess the fear. People tell me that their fear is irrational, but I always help them dig into the details. Sometimes there is a kernel of truth that feeds the fear.

2. If the fear is substantiated, problem-solve worst-case scenarios. Problem-solving worst-case scenarios shows that we can survive bad outcomes.

3. If the fear is not substantiated, it is likely an artifact of past bad experiences. Talk it through with a supportive friend.

4. Rely on an objective perspective of someone you trust. I told one of my clients to remind himself that his brain was playing tricks on him. He was able to lean intellectually on this assessment until the emotion subsided.

5. Acknowledge when fear reveals positive movement. Discomfort makes us feel like something is wrong, such that we interpret it as fear. Sometimes fear is a sign that we have moved out of our comfort zone to pursue something special.

6. Remember that fear is not a fact. It is a feeling. You can determine how seriously you are going to take it.

7. If you are fearful in general and tend to worry a lot, you may be struggling with generalized anxiety disorder. This problem is prevalent and solvable. Seek out a trained professional to walk you through it.

ANGER

In my doctoral program, we recorded our client appointments and periodically reviewed them on video. In one situation, I worked with a group of people in which one person was potentially suicidal. I interjected some humor to lessen the anxiety of the group so we could work effectively. The student-supervisor later reviewed a few minutes of the video at the exact segment when I had used humor as a tool. Based on 10% of the information available, she concluded that I struggled with empathy and had not taken the problem seriously. I remember feeling angry at the insult and, underneath of that anger, fear. I felt helpless that someone in power could make incorrect assumptions about my expertise.

Hurt and fear make us feel vulnerable, but anger makes us feel strong. "You're a jerk" feels safer than "I'm afraid that you don't love me." It feels better to say, "This organization is ridiculous" instead of "I'm scared that I'm going to get fired." If we can acknowledge the underlying emotions of anger, we can develop effective coping strategies. If we simply focus on the anger, the underlying emotions will prolong the problem.

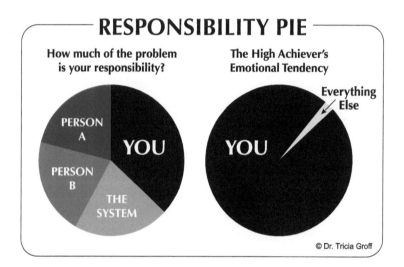

RESPONSIBILITY PIE

How much of the problem is your responsibility?

PERSON A
PERSON B
THE SYSTEM
YOU

The High Achiever's Emotional Tendency

YOU
Everything Else

© Dr. Tricia Groff

Anger at Ourselves versus Anger at Others

"Are you angrier at him or yourself?" I ask this question when my clients are in an anger vortex that they can't escape. Many of us are the angriest when we are blaming ourselves for part of the situation. I often try to figure out the degree to which I am angry toward myself versus someone else. Owning my slice of responsibility gives me control over what I can change the next time. This strategy does not mean that we should own the whole responsibility pie. High achievers have a propensity for assuming too much responsibility, and so the trick is to step back and objectively evaluate the factors of the situation.

Anger as a Tool

While anger can mask hurt or fear, it also acts as a powerful warning indicator for system problems. Stress, fatigue, and schedule overload potentiate anger. Manipulative, disrespectful, and ungrateful people create anger. Depression feeds anger. However, even with all of these negative inputs, anger can be a powerful tool for change.

I always get excited when nice people get angry, because I know they will take action. They will fire an unhelpful employee, draw the boundary with the relative who is mooching money, or snap back at the insulting colleague instead of "taking the high road." I recently became enraged when I witnessed racial targeting, and my reaction reminded me that anger at injustice fuels social change.

How to Use Anger to Create Change

First, figure out why you are angry.

1.   Are you angry at yourself or other people?

2. Is there hurt, fear, disappointment, or other emotions mixed with the anger?

3. Are you angry because someone took advantage of you?

4. Are you angry because someone challenged your core values?

5. Are you angry because someone assassinated your character?

6. Are you angry because you've allowed bad behavior?

7. Are you angry on behalf of others?

8. Are you angry at processes?

Next, figure out what needs to change. For example, if someone took advantage of you, what will you do differently to keep that from happening again? If someone assassinated your character, how can you distance yourself in that relationship? If someone habitually misbehaves, will you stop tolerating the behavior, or do you need to lower your expectations?

Let's talk about processes for a second. Anger and frustration are closely intertwined. In the same way that fear and hurt often drive anger, so does frustration. When we want to achieve a goal, and encounter a barrier, we become frustrated. When the source of frustration is a faulty process or someone else's incompetence, we often become angry.

If you dread part of your work process, assess whether you can change or eliminate it. Maybe you thrive on developing strategy, but you abhor administration. Ensure that you don't waste time coping with frustration when you could eliminate the source of it.

At one point in my career, I contracted with insurance companies to offer counseling. I found I wasted a lot of time compensating for their mistakes. Whether I spent 30 minutes or two hours on the problem, the anger tainted my day. I lowered my expectations of competence, yet I was still frustrated. So I stopped accepting their contracts. My anger immediately disappeared.

Using Anger to Get Others to Take You Seriously

Controlled and nonreactive anger helps people take us seriously. First, let me remind you of what *not* to do. **Do not say or do things from a position of reactive anger, especially in work contexts.** It will hurt you or make others take you less seriously. We may write, say, or do things that we can't take back. In the best-case scenario, you show your cards too early and lose power. Worst case, the other person wins—twice. The first win is that they made you angry. The second win is that their behavior caused you to write an email that makes you look bad to everyone. *(Note: I use the term "showing cards" throughout out this book. It means giving people information that they can use against us.)*

In highly complex political scenarios, a moment of anger can tear apart months or years of work. Sometimes winning the war means using anger to fuel you internally without breaking a sweat externally. You can break the calm facade after, and only after, you have thoroughly assessed the situation, have a plan, and have covered your posterior in every direction.

In lower-stakes scenarios, masking anger can also be problematic if we want people to take us seriously. Some of us conceal anger because we don't want to hurt people's feelings or lose control. Many of us appropriately control our anger in professional interactions. Unfortunately, some people only respond when they hear a certain tone of voice. Thus, it is helpful for us to know how to use controlled anger effectively. Some guidelines:

1. Allow just enough of an angry edge to get someone's attention. Remember, if you lose control, you lose power.

2. Experiment with the three-strikes rule. Use calm rationale the first time, add firmness for the second request, and allow the edge to come out the third time.

3. If you need to use anger to get someone's attention, assess whether this is a one-time interaction or if you will have continual contact. Engaging with someone who only responds to anger will drain you.

Use controlled anger sparingly and only if you follow up with congruent action. A lot of people push down anger. Pressure builds, and they "blow up." The emotion diminishes, and everyone assumes that things are back to normal. Nothing changes because no problem-solving occurred. Frequent angry outbursts yield diminishing returns. If a patient person gets angry once per year, the people around him or her will take the situation seriously. On the other hand, when someone gets angry each week, he or she is viewed as emotionally volatile and is dismissed accordingly.

FRUSTRATION

"I want to help this division succeed, but no one gets back to me."
"This employee has potential, but he doesn't seem motivated to try."
"I just want people to act like adults."
—Quotes from frustrated high achievers in leadership

If you have any type of ambition or desire for excellence, you will be frustrated. The most common source of frustration in high achievers is the mismatch between the way we think the world should work and the reality at hand. If you are competent, you will be frustrated because the efforts of others will continually disappoint you. If you are logical, you will be flummoxed by decisions that seem irrational. If you value fairness and integrity, you will be confused when others do not act from those principles. Since you value excellence, you will want others to value it too. You'll want to help people grow, but sometimes, you will feel that you care more about their success than they do. If you are a high achiever, you will always have high expectations of yourself and others, regardless of whether there is evidence to support those expectations. If you can cultivate awareness that your high expectations will clash with the constraints at hand, you'll be one step closer to mastering frustration.

What to Do with Frustration

1. Figure out exactly why you are frustrated.

2. When you are frustrated with another person, understand that you can work around people, but you can't change them. Accepting this fact will help you to adjust your effort and expectations, thus reducing the frustration.

3. Expect things to go wrong. The higher the number of variables in any project, the higher the likelihood that something will go wrong. Build margins to accommodate potential problems. This tactic reduces time-related stress.

4. Lower your expectations about everything and everybody. You don't need to lower your standards or think negatively. You do need to base your expectations on the evidence at hand rather than what you think **should** happen.

5. Expect incompetence to occur at whatever frequency you believe is average. Use a tally system to track when it happens. Over time, incompetence will be less shocking, which will lower your emotional reactivity to it. Sometimes you will be pleasantly surprised to have weeks without incompetence, which allows you to see that the bigger picture balances out.

6. Stop doing the same thing and expecting different results. If you had a conversation with someone about the same

problem three times, why would a fourth conversation make a difference?

7. Get an outside perspective to help you see patterns that you may not be able to see.

8. For frustrating tasks or problem-solving, you'll get further by taking a break or switching to another project.

9. Physical activity can create that moment of insight that cracks a case. Sometimes taking a break from active problem-solving saves us time and energy while still achieving our desired outcome. (For my neuroscience geeks, we are quieting the dorsolateral prefrontal cortex and allowing the cerebellum to play. The prefrontal cortex controls cognitive activities, and the cerebellum facilitates creativity.)

10. Let the people around you know that you are frustrated, but not with them. They will often provide emotional support or brainstorm solutions.

Script: "I'm not frustrated with you; I'm just annoyed with the whole situation."

Sometimes the most frustrating part of frustration is that it combines with other emotions. Imagine that you are trying to resolve a conflict in a significant relationship. The conversation is circular, and you can't seem to "get through." The frustration may combine with hurt from harsh words or concern that the other person doesn't understand you. You may feel hopeless because you've had the same conversation before. If your emotions are a jumbled mess, acknowledge that you are frustrated. It may take a few days for you to understand your feelings.

> **Script:** "I'm frustrated that we are having this same conversation again, but I'm sure that you are frustrated too. Can we look at it from a different angle?"

Before you move on to learning about disappointment, copy strategies 1 to 6 and put them at your desk. Rewrite them or use your own words. Adjusting your expectations will prevent anger, frustration, and disappointment.

DISAPPOINTMENT

"I don't want to hope, Dr. Tricia. The disappointment is crushing."
—From a business owner

Maybe someone you respected disappointed you. Maybe you had a dream, and losing it crushed you. For some people, disappointments run deep, far back into childhood, when life gradually eroded their faith that good things could happen.

People who have been repeatedly disappointed struggle to engage in new opportunities or relationships fully. We try to protect ourselves from disappointment by not "getting our hopes up." Logically, this strategy makes sense, but it doesn't help us emotionally. We automatically hope, and hope is a good thing. Hope provides resilience and allows us to thrive, even after we've been defeated.

In the same way that I believe hurt feelings will happen if we have relationships, I believe disappointment will happen if we are successful. If we strive, we reach for opportunities that are not guaranteed outcomes. We take personal and professional risks to optimize the potential upsides. Our goals are ridiculously large, because we know that we will achieve more if we aim beyond what is reasonable. Thus, we are more likely to endure disappointment than if we were to remain satisfied with the status quo.

Statistical Hope

If you continue to try new strategies, tactics, or thought processes, you'll likely get a win instead of a disappointment. You know this logically, but it takes guts to keep the faith. When people start businesses, friendships, or hobbies, they often give up too early. My pet peeve is when someone with great potential says, "Well, I tried that once, and it didn't work." If what you tried was jumping off a cliff, maybe it's a good idea to stop. However, if you have a larger and more complicated endeavor, assess the contributing variables to determine whether to change the strategy or let go of the effort.

How to Cope with Disappointment

1. Acknowledge the loss.

2. Talk with your friends.

3. Journal.

4. Identify items for which you are grateful.

5. Trust in time to ease the sting.

6. Assess if you need to change any processes to avoid a recurrence.

Learning how to cope with disappointment allows us to tenaciously pursue our goals. At the same time, it's helpful to be aware of actions that cause disappointment, lest you create a self-fulfilling prophecy of negative outcomes.

How to Guarantee Disappointment

Two great strategies guarantee disappointment:

1. Do the same thing and expect different results.

2. Set your expectations on what you think "should" be true without accommodating the variables of the actual people and situations at hand.

Sometimes our good intentions guarantee disappointment. We may want to give someone the benefit of the doubt, remain optimistic, or make sure that we are not quitting. Perhaps we try to get emotional support from someone who is selfish. Maybe the market for a business idea is dwindling, but we are reluctant to pivot. We may try to salvage a personal or business relationship, even when all flags point to "exit."

High achievers are especially vulnerable to guaranteeing disappointment because we think the best of people, and we are problem-solvers. Thus, we spend an inordinate amount of time trying to change others and attempting to fix entrenched systems of dysfunction.

The problem with continued attachment to a positive outcome is that we cannot adapt in the face of contradictory evidence. If we set our expectations for what we want to be true, rather than according to what is accurate, we stay stuck. On the other hand, if we set our expectations according to the evidence in front of us, we can adapt our strategy and obtain a better outcome. It may not be our preferred outcome. However, the result will still be better than perpetual disappointment.

LONELINESS

There are a lot of possible emotions to discuss, and I chose the ones that I help people problem-solve most frequently...except this one. People don't talk about loneliness. Loneliness is possibly the most painful emotion because it results from a rupture between our present existence and our fundamental human need to belong. My clients usually don't tell me that they feel lonely. They use a phrase that meshes loneliness with the fear of being enough. "Is this normal?" they ask me.

What they mean is "Does this happen to other people or am I alone in this problem? Is something wrong with me?" Many people feel lonely because they don't hear anyone else talk about the issues they face. Thus, it's easy to assume that they are the only one experiencing the problem.

Loneliness also occurs when we think we don't belong with other people. In chapter 1, I mentioned that high achievers may have had difficulty fitting in with their social groups. Alternately, you may have moved a lot when you were young, creating an ongoing feeling of being on the outside.

Leadership can add to this feeling of being "other." One of my clients noted that he doesn't have peers with whom he can share challenges. In young businesses, solo founders bear the decision-making weight alone. For innovative leaders, the same outside-the-box thinking that fosters success fuels loneliness.

I know that it can be hard to find people with similar mindsets. Statistically, you may be in the minority. Yet all of us have more in common with other people than we think. As soon as we can recognize that even in our differences we are not that unique, we can focus on how we belong. You don't have to be an extrovert to use the tips below. Most of us need only one or two people in our quarter to help us feel that we are not alone.

How to Deal with Loneliness

1. When you meet people with similarly high standards of purpose, integrity, and performance, prioritize the relationship.

2. When you meet people, look for what you have in common instead of focusing on the differences.

3. If you want to meet people with whom you can connect, start a special-interest group.

4. Talk about the things that bother you. You'll be shocked by the number of people who experience the same problem.

5. Reach out to help. Send a note, make a call, or give a kind word to a stranger.

6. Serve in your communities or with causes about which you care. These endeavors help us to meet like-minded people, providing the purpose and connection we crave.

7. Allow your mistakes to connect you. As high achievers, we want to be superior in our excellence; we cringe and feel inferior when we falter. If humans make mistakes and you are human, is it possible that you belong more than you think you do?

In this chapter, we focused on the negative emotions that drain us. While specific tactics are appropriate for each emotion, the following list of strategies will increase your coping skills across all emotions.

RECOMMENDATIONS FOR ALL EMOTIONS

1. **Find Healthy Coping Strategies**. I love it when people say they don't want to have a crutch when, in reality, we all do. A crutch is something you lean on when you feel weak. Choose a crutch that makes you feel better without inducing a literal or metaphorical hangover. Some options include talking with friends, exercising,

• EMOTIONS–I KNOW YOU WANT TO SKIP THEM •

praying or meditating, writing, and reading encouraging books. Some of my clients love video games; others work on cars.

I know that some of you are asking how much alcohol or how much weed is okay. The answer depends on the rest of your pattern. Is it occasional or for fun? Or is it the only thing you have to look forward to each day? If it's the latter, you'll be happier and more successful by problem-solving the source of stress.

2. **Exercise.** Exercise can instantly lift one's mood during daily struggles and provides a sound foundation for longer-term mood management. If you are a high achiever who is juggling multiple demands, you can't afford to skip exercising.

3. **Breathe.** Why does breathing help? When we are anxious or stressed, our sympathetic nervous system turns on. Think of the fight-or-flight mechanism. When we are relaxed, the parasympathetic nervous system is in play. The two systems are mutually exclusive—you can't turn both on at the same time. Deep breathing is associated with the parasympathetic nervous system. Think of watching someone you love when they are sleeping. Their stomach moves up and down. When we breathe deeply, we activate the parasympathetic nervous system, making it difficult for us to sustain high arousal, thus lowering our stress.

4. **Sleep.** Fatigue will always exacerbate negative emotions. Don't waste time analyzing your emotions at bedtime, because you will usually feel significantly different in the morning. Sleep is critical to our psychological functioning and ongoing emotional balance.

5. **Assess Antecedents.** A lot of people get upset without spending the time to figure out the antecedents of their emotions. If you can understand the variables that impact you, you find solutions and gain power over your emotional state. This week, two of my clients were highly stressed, and they didn't know why. We assessed the antecedents. It turned out that they were just "peopled out"—introverts who had too many people engagements in one week. We looked at their schedules and planned alone time. It was that simple.

6. **Be Aware of Lag Time.** Some people are aware of their emotions and can name them immediately; other people simply know that they are upset but have no idea why. If you have emotional lag time, predict it and be patient with it. You *will* be able to figure out what you are feeling; you may just need extra time.

7. **Talk to Someone.** Talk to someone you trust when your emotions are in chaos. Someone else can often put words and context to the emotion. This outside perspective helps us to gain clarity and feel less alone.

8. **Practice Tolerating Emotion.** It's okay to be grumpy for a day. None of us wants to feel that way, but it happens.

9. **Distract Yourself.** If you are struggling with intense emotion, set a timer and allow yourself to feel the emotion. Then do something else that requires focus. Some people play video games; others read. You want an activity that demands attention and distracts you from the problem.

10. **Focus on Tasks and Goals That Are Under Your Control.** Sometimes it's hard to focus when we are emotional, and then we get upset because we are not productive. Keep a list of tasks that you can do even if you are upset. Write down what you accomplish. It won't solve the emotional problem, but it will help you feel productive.

11. **Figure Out Where You Feel Emotions in Your Body.** So far, my clients have said their chest, stomach, head, and hands. When you figure out where you feel the emotion, train yourself to be more attuned to that part of your body. Sometimes we note the physical changes in our bodies before we register the feelings. In these cases, early physiological recognition can aid real-time decision-making and help us identify the emotion's antecedents.

12. **Resolve Recurring, Triggering Situations**. When a person or situation is repeatedly triggering an emotion, take it seriously. You can't simply decide that it won't bother you. Yes, there are cognitive techniques that we can use to change our perceptions; however, we will have better success by resolving a recurring situation.

13. **Journal**. Over the years, even nonwriter clients have said, "I wrote this out, and it helped." Writing forces mental chaos into a sequence that allows us to gain insight.

14. **Remember Why You Care**. Maybe you view life as a video game that you want to win. Or maybe life is a sacred contract, informed by your spiritual beliefs. Be aware of how you make meaning. When life is hard and we are overwhelmed, we all fare better if we can answer one question: "Why am I doing this?"

In this chapter, we focused on common negative emotions. The next chapter will help you prevent the emotional imbalances that create resentment, stress, emotional exhaustion, and emotional burnout.

KEY TAKEAWAYS

1. *Emotion doesn't make you weak; it makes you human.*

2. *You can't out-think emotion.*

3. *Identify the antecedents of your emotional responses so that you can adjust your future expectations and actions.*

LEADERSHIP APPLICATION

1. You will not be able to build loyalty without addressing other people's emotions. The only way that other people will share their feelings is when you share some of your own. Words like "transparency," "vulnerability," and "authenticity" are more easily said than lived. Underlying all of these concepts is the courageous decision to deal with emotion instead of running from it. There is no shortcut.

2. As you get better at identifying your own emotions, you increase your ability to recognize the feelings of others. People trust us when they feel that their emotions are heard and understood. That trust increases decision-making speed, fosters openness to change, and optimizes business deals. You will have a ceiling on your leadership and professional success if you choose to operate apart from emotion.

3. If you are having a tough day, let the team know whether your emotions are related to a task at hand or something else. You don't have to give details, but you must address it. People feel your emotion, even when you think that you are hiding it. A simple acknowledgment that you are "off" today

can allay the anxiety and unease that occurs when others sense a problem.

4. Increasing your ability to differentiate your own emotions (angry versus frustrated) will help you use feeling words in your interactions with others. The use of feeling words is the basis of verbal empathy. Verbal empathy (such as saying, "It must be frustrating...") helps people open up and give you more information than you could have obtained with any other strategy. Verbal empathy is the basis of high-stakes negotiation. (Check out a great book called *Never Split the Difference*, by Chris Voss.)

5. If you are trying to change an individual's perspective or create change in an organization, you must identify and account for the emotions involved. If you attempt to use logical arguments to resolve emotionally charged situations, you will lose the trust of those around you.

Chapter 4

EMOTIONAL
IMBALANCES

E motions require energy. That's why they're annoying sometimes,
right? In the previous chapter, we discussed specific emotions.
In this chapter, we'll focus on emotional energy imbalances.
Resentment, emotional vomit, stress, and emotional burnout result
from problems in the emotional exchange system. Resentment
occurs when we give more than we get back, creating an emotional
deficit. Emotional vomit is the spewing of excess emotion on others,
exhausting the recipients. Stress and overwhelm occur when situational demands outstrip our coping resources. Burnout results from
prolonged emotional output without adequate refueling. Each of
these phenomena drains us emotionally and adversely impacts our

relationships. The prevention and adjustment strategies below will help you maintain emotional equilibrium.

RESENTMENT

"Can I have some referrals?" I asked my attorney friend. "I just turned down business partners, and I want to send them some resources. They wanted me to help them fix the relationship, but the relationship is irretrievably broken. They are going to get divorced; they just don't know it yet." You see, apart from the business logistics at hand, I had heard resentment in both of their voices.

Resentment is an imbalance between what we put into a relationship and what we expect to receive. The imbalance creates a little leak. It seems easier to ignore the leak than to address it, until the day we open the cupboard door and find poisonous black mold. The leak starts when people hurt, disrespect, or take advantage of us. Egregious acts may end the relationship, but less salient injuries create a slow leak under the sink. We want to give people the benefit of the doubt and move on. We want to close the cupboard door and hope that the leak goes away. We might say statements like these:

- "I don't want to make things worse."

- "I don't want to end the relationship."

- "It's not a big deal; I just need to accept it."

We say this so we don't have to face what's there. But when we allow the leak to continue, we guarantee black mold.

I predict the end of relationships with a fair amount of accuracy. It's not because I have extrasensory foreknowledge. Rather, when I hear resentment, I understand the toxicity of it. The length of time, the amount of investment, and the amount of loss varies, but the end result remains the same. Resentment kills relationships.

When you address the leak early on, you have a chance to save the relationship. You will have more emotional resources to pursue the best outcome. One of my clients experienced this with a new hire. A month after hiring her, he texted me, *She is criticizing me as well as the team. I am already feeling resentful. I have to confront her.* We planned a script, and he had a conversation with her. Her behavior changed, and the resentment receded. The conversation may have saved her job.

If you like to think the best of people, expect others to treat you as you treat them, dislike conflict, and try to go the extra mile, you are especially vulnerable to resentment. You will go into relationships with the best of intentions, give more than you should, and wait to address your frustration. You will hang on to the hope that the situation or the person will change.

If you wait to have difficult conversations, the resentment will build as your emotional resources recede. By the time everything comes to a head, reconciliation will not be an option. If you are engaged in any type of high-consequence relationship, whether it is a business partnership, an investor relationship, or a marriage relationship, a simple conversation when you first notice the leak may save the relationship (and maybe millions of dollars).

Tips to Prevent Resentment

1. **Have direct conversations about your expectations at the beginning of an engagement.** Elucidating what you consider "common sense" helps to clarify discrepancies in expectations at the onset. The initial discussion paves the way for additional conversations if a conflict occurs.

2. **Be honest with yourself about relationship fit.** It's easy to ignore the red flags when we see the opportunity in a relationship. This intentional blindness happens in business relationships and often costs more than the value of the opportunity.

3. **Create a system for catching leaks early in both personal and professional relationships.** Incorporate a weekly or biweekly touching-base routine to discuss updates. The habit allows us to address frustration before it turns into resentment. It also allows us to systemize successes, lending a balanced and productive feel to the conversations.

Script: "What worked well for us this week? Is there any place where we went off course or any systems we need to change?"

4. **Don't make exceptions to your boundaries to please people.** Clear boundaries and expectations protect relationships. You can't maintain positive energy if you are resentful. When we cross our boundaries to "be nice," we sow seeds of resentment.

5. **If you ignore the advice of number 4 and make an exception, do not expect appreciation for your effort.** This advice sounds harsh, but the truth is, most people don't know the amount of effort we've expended to make exceptions. We have an assumption about the amount of appreciation that should occur when we make a sacrifice. We get angry and disappointed if people are not appreciative. We think, *After everything I did for this person...* The problem with this thought process is that the other person may not be aware of our sacrifice. So whose fault is it? **Whenever we stretch beyond what feels appropriate, we increase the risk of resentment.** We may want to blame them for our feelings, but we started the leak. If we accept the fact that we have responsibility in preventing resentment, we are better able to set boundaries and appropriate expectations.

6. **Give the amount that feels good or adjust the giving ratio.** In psychology, there are two unpalatable yet critical concepts about relationships. One is social exchange theory, which posits that people weigh relationships according to the costs and benefits. We try to maximize the benefits of a relationship and minimize the costs. While the concept may sound mercenary, we automatically do this with no ill intentions. Don't you like the relationships in which you are able to have fun with fairly little effort? Compare that feeling to relationships with people you love, but who are high maintenance. Did you ever spend extra time finding

a lunch meeting place that is convenient for you and the other person, instead of simply driving the extra distance to his location?

A related concept is called social equity theory. Social equity theory posits that if we are in social exchange relationships, we want to ensure that the relationships are fair. We subconsciously calculate and compare the input/output ratios of people in a relationship to see if everyone is getting the same amount out of the relationship for the amount that they put in. We can easily understand this if we think about how business partners assess equity. *Is my slice of the pie appropriate for the amount that I'm investing?* It sounds nice to say that we don't keep score, but most people expect reciprocity in a relationship. When the outcome is less than expected, the ratio is unbalanced, and resentment occurs.

Giving credence to these theories means that we accept that we are more likely to feel resentment if we do not see a lot of benefit in the relationship and/or if we feel that our efforts are greater than the other person's efforts, with no increased return.

Decreasing the amount of effort is one of the ways that we can rebalance the equation. Sometimes my well-intentioned clients debate me about the suggestion to reduce effort. They say that they want to stay consistent, regardless of the other person's actions: "I want to take the higher road. I want to be generous regardless of the other person's behavior." Then they get resentful and angry when the other person continues to disappoint them.

7. **Terminate relationships.** Adjusting the ratio is a short-term solution in a professional environment. High achievers hate giving less. Discuss separation when you see problems in basic alignment. Address painful conversations early to increase the possibility of a thoughtful and respectful separation.

LEADERSHIP APPLICATION

Black mold can spread through teams, so remember that terminating relationships helps maintain the health of an organization.

EMOTIONAL VOMIT

Emotional vomit happens when we are overflowing with negative emotions, and "we just have to get it out." Our emotions are imbalanced, and so we take the excess emotion and put it on someone else. When our unsuspecting spouse, friend, or colleague is the sudden recipient of overwhelming anger, fear, or sadness, we are vomiting on them. They haven't done anything wrong, and suddenly, they are covered in our emotions.

People are differentially affected by someone else's emotional vomit. Some individuals can say, "It's someone else's emotion; it has nothing to do with me." Others will feel exhausted from the weight of emotion. Communicating about the emotional vomit—where it's coming from and what you need—helps to mitigate the negative impact on the people around you.

© Dr. Tricia Groff

Emotional Vomit

Sometimes you want to vomit emotions on someone who has wronged you. People have said to me, "Tricia, I just want to let them know exactly how I feel." If you do this, you lose all power in the situation. Venting anger or frustration, just to "get it out," will give the adversary information that can be used against you or will cause you to say things you don't mean to someone you love. Both of those possibilities jeopardize your ability to ensure a positive long-term outcome.

When you feel the need to vent, figure out if you want to speak to a trusted friend or if it is better to use a professional. In high-stakes situations, even trusted friends or colleagues may inadvertently comment on something you said in confidence. In these situations, seek a professional who can handle the emotion and provide the confidentiality so you have a safe place to vent.

How to Vent without Covering People in Vomit

1. **Monitor the time frame.** If you need to vent, help the other person know that there is a time limit.

Script: "I just need to vent to you for 20 minutes. Then we can change topics."

2. **Tell them how they can help.** When people know what you need, it will help them to relax and be present with you.

Script Options:

   a. "I just need to vent for 5 minutes. You don't need to problem-solve or do anything. I just need to get it out."

   b. "I'm so frustrated with this situation. Can you tell me if I'm missing something?"

   c. "This situation hit my insecurity button. I need reassurance."

   d. "I don't know what I need, or if even if I need anything. I just need to say this out loud."

3. **Use words.** Emotional vomit happens even when you aren't speaking. If you read the paragraph on emotional vomit

and thought, *That doesn't apply to me because I don't speak when I'm upset*, then you may be the worst offender. **If you radiate negative emotion, but say nothing about it or deny that there is a problem, you make people anxious and unsettled.** You don't need to go into details; a simple explanation will help them to relax.

Script Options:

a. "I'm frustrated, but I don't want to talk about it yet. I'll fill you in when I calm down."

b. "I'm frustrated. I don't know if I want to talk about it, but I'll let you know if that would be helpful."

c. "I'm upset, and I don't want to take it out on anyone. I just need a little bit of space."

Protective Strategies for People with High Empathy

Special reminder: Skip this section, unless you struggle to manage extreme empathy where you take on other people's feelings as though they are your own. An empath is a person who self-describes as ultrasensitive to others' emotions. It is not an official diagnostic category, but you can research the term online and learn more about people with whom this categorization resonates.

I had just met the spouse of a colleague, and we dropped right into the conversation about being a magnet for emotional vomit. My new acquaintance noted that her husband had bought her a shirt that says, "Please talk to me. I'll be your therapist." The downside of being empathetic is that even strangers may sense your compassion and dump on you. If you have extremely high levels of empathy, such that you can feel another person's emotions as if they are happening to you, emotional vomit can be draining and painful. Here are some suggestions on how to protect yourself:

1. **Give yourself permission to abstain from being a receptacle for someone else's pain.** You need to conserve your emotional energy for yourself and the people who are already in your circle.

2. **Be careful about whom you bring into your sphere in the first place.** People who are unable to contain their emotional vomit will be toxic to you.

3. **Prevent vomit from strangers and acquaintances by doing the *opposite* of what you usually do.** What opens the floodgates of others' emotions:

   a. Smiling (I'm approachable)

   b. Eye contact (I'm interested)

   c. "How are you?" (I'll be your captive audience)

d. Empathy (Any statement of understanding that includes emotion words such as "frustrated," "sad," or "stressed")

So...

a. Don't smile on approach.

b. Half-smile to strangers. (I'm friendly but not open enough for you to approach me.)

c. Limit eye contact.

d. Keep responses vague. "I'm sorry to hear that; I hope things get better for you," rather than, "That sounds frustrating."

4. **Imagine a plexiglas shield between you and the other person.** Imagine that the words are coming at you but bouncing off of the plexiglass and dripping down. This technique helps to protect you, but you can still hear what the other person is saying.

5. **Imagine that the vomiter has swallowed helium and is talking in a squeaky voice.**

6. **Pray or repeat affirmations.** The internal dialogue will provide a subtle distraction and buffer you against inhaling the person's emotion.

7. **Talk yourself through it.** There are many times that
    I simply repeat, "This is X's emotion; I don't have to
    have it."

8. **Sometimes people do not verbally vomit, but you can still
    feel the emotion in their bodies.** Try to tune in enough
    to recognize when this is happening. One time, my neck
    started hurting, and I realized that I felt my client's neck
    pain. I said to myself, "It's his pain, Tricia. You don't have
    to hurt." I instantly felt better, asked if he got headaches,
    and began problem-solving the pain instead of taking it on
    myself. I recognize when this is happening because the pain
    seems to come out of nowhere and only starts during the
    interaction with the other person.

9. **Become adept at distracting the vomiter and changing
    topics.**

10. **Make sure that you have exit strategies for potentially
    draining conversations or situations.** Exit strategies may
    involve having your own transportation, a meeting you
    have to attend, or a designated friend to rescue you.

There is nothing magical about these protection techniques. You
want to recognize when you are consuming someone else's pain or
anxiety, then use imagery, distraction, or self-talk to help create a
buffer against ingesting the other person's emotions.

EMOTIONAL BURNOUT

"I want to walk away," he told his wife. My client repeated the conversation that had transpired prior to him seeking executive coaching. Even though he was passionate about his organization, he was emotionally bankrupt and physically empty. He barely had enough energy to get through the day, became angry easily, and had difficulty finding joy in what had been his calling.

Two years later, he stood in the kitchen, and his wife looked at him. "You're noticeably different," she said. "What strategies do you and Tricia discuss?" I laughed as my client recounted the conversation, and I waited for his answer. Frankly, I have a hard time explaining what I do, so I was curious to see what he had told his wife. His answer: "Well, it's hard to explain. I guess I would say that she helps me understand how I'm wired, what drains me, what fuels me, and how to prioritize. She also helps me manage the drains." It sounds like a simple formula, but if you are a leader with ever-evolving responsibilities, you have an ongoing tension between the overflow of items demanding your attention and the amount of energy you have to give to them.

Emotional burnout occurs when we use emotional energy without replenishing it. Motivation, relationships, self-discipline, conflict, even excitement—all of these use our emotional resources. Like physical energy, emotional energy is finite. It needs to be recharged, just as food and sleep increase physical energy.

Imagine trying to drive a car on a dead battery, just because you think it should work. You wouldn't do that, would you? High achievers do precisely that. It's easy to assume that our resources are limitless. Our desire to excel compounds our magical thinking, and so we drive without recharging. We think that human limitations are for everyone else until we start burning out through fatigue, anxiety, inflammation, or heart problems.

The way to avoid burnout is to track your energy fuels and drains. Common examples of fuels include reading, biking, alone time, time with spouse or friends, meditation/spiritual time, or time in nature. Examples of drains include relational conflict, work stress, parenting worry, frequent task switching, lack of alone time, multiple significant life changes in a short period, stagnation, and grief.

I often ask my analytical clients to add numerical ratings. The precision helps them to understand the most effective fuels and the most significant source of energy drains.

Real Client Chart of Fuels and Drains

Fuels at Work

High-Level Modeling	+3
Business Development	+2
Marketing Strategy	+3
Employee Strategy	+2

Drains at Work

Email Overload	−1
Tedious Reporting	−3
Employee Discipline	−3
Constant Interruptions	−2

It is helpful to recognize the drains that rapidly deplete us. I experience rapid drain if I am worried about someone or if I need to navigate a high-stakes situation. When we know the stressors that cause our energy to tank the fastest, we can temporarily cut off other activities to conserve energy. Further, we can problem-solve those areas to prevent or ameliorate future drains. In my experience, relational stress drains people fast. It's the reason I'm so passionate about the need to be discriminating on who we bring into our sphere in the first place.

When our emotional output is greater than the fuel available, we lose the buffer to adjust to additional challenges. "Buffer" is the energy reserve that allows us to deal with unanticipated problems without burning out. People in gas-consuming vehicles know there is a little reserve in the tank, even when the meter shows empty. That's buffer.

When we do not refuel, we lose buffer. As our buffer wears thin, we may be edgy, impatient, or feel that even fun tasks are additional burdens. When we have no buffer and continue our energy output, we go into a redlining state. At this point, our body begins to compensate, and we notice chronic fatigue, inflammatory markers, digestive issues, and the exacerbation of preexisting medical conditions. It is usually in this red-lining state that people recognize burnout.

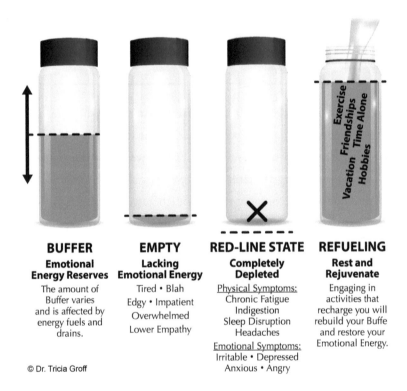

BUFFER	EMPTY	RED-LINE STATE	REFUELING
Emotional Energy Reserves	**Lacking Emotional Energy**	**Completely Depleted**	**Rest and Rejuvenate**
The amount of Buffer varies and is affected by energy fuels and drains.	Tired • Blah Edgy • Impatient Overwhelmed Lower Empathy	<u>Physical Symptoms:</u> Chronic Fatigue Indigestion Sleep Disruption Headaches <u>Emotional Symptoms:</u> Irritable • Depressed Anxious • Angry	Engaging in activities that recharge you will rebuild your Buffer and restore your Emotional Energy.

© Dr. Tricia Groff

To sustain excellence, you must be super-attentive to the energy input/output ratio. Since you tend to go above and beyond, handle crises well, and take care of others, there is a tendency to underestimate the actual amount of buffer available. When we can chart our fuels and drains, and manage the amount of buffer we have, we can prioritize our activities to prevent burnout.

Strategies to Prevent and Address Emotional Burnout

1. **Expect that changing your patterns may be physically uncomfortable.** Years ago, I was on vacation. I couldn't relax with my novel, even though I had been excited about reading brain candy. Finally, I went up to the guest room and opened my computer. I immediately felt my heart rate slow down and my body relax. Why? Because I had trained myself at a neurological level that working all the time was normal.

2. **Do a rapid detox.** If work feels more comfortable than relaxing, practice what I call "rapid detox." Force yourself to do nothing—whether it's for 2 hours or 2 days. By "nothing," I mean that it can't be productive. If you have neurologically conditioned yourself to be more comfortable working than relaxing, this tactic feels excruciating. You'll feel like jumping out of your skin. If you can stay with the discomfort, you'll start to feel your body relax. How long does it take? It depends on your personality and level of burnout. It can take several days to feel a difference. Many of you will not have several days, so work with smaller time blocks first. Options of what to do in rapid detox include noneducational movies, fishing, woodworking, novels, flying, meditation...anything that helps you debrief your brain.

3. **Formulate a delegation pathway.**

a. **Make a complete list of the tasks and areas of responsibility that drain you.** One of my clients didn't know where to start with this suggestion, so I asked him to review his emails with me. This technique provided us with a starting point of what was on his plate in the first place. Often, we move fast and juggle responsibilities such that we underestimate the number of items we address in a day.

b. **Which of those tasks need to be completed with 100% accuracy? 80% accuracy? 70% accuracy?** Since you are a high achiever, you may be delegating to someone less skilled than you. What is the level of competence that satisfies the essential requirements?

c. **Make a list of the people to whom you can delegate.** Make sure the fit is right, and train people to your expectations. Otherwise, you will get frustrated and revert to doing the tasks yourself. If you say, "I have no one who can do this," the gaps in available skillsets will inform your training and hiring decisions.

d. **Assess what you want the big picture to look like a few years out.** What are the key areas of responsibility that fuel you *and* contribute the highest value to the organization? When you answer that question, you can start backing into a sequence of the people you need and the order in which you should start delegating.

4. **Fire people.** I'm sorry. I know I'm making it sound much too easy. One Difficult Person seems to create the same drain as all other stressors combined.

5. **Get clear about what constitutes an emergency.** Is anyone dying?

6. **Practice self-discipline.** Train yourself to step away from the email, the laptop, or the phone in the same way that you step away from candy. Set appropriate precedents with yourself and others to help you control the pattern of 24/7 availability. Remember that none of this is comfortable in the beginning.

7. **Get an accountability partner.** I hate the term "accountability partner" because it brings out my psychological reactance. It works. I know this because clients send me pictures of themselves fishing, reading, and hiking. It is code for "see, I'm listening." A good accountability partner will understand that you crave both excellence and balance. They need to "get" you.

8. **Distinguish between your wishes and your nonnegotiables.** When you feel your buffer getting thin, pare down your schedule to what is absolutely necessary. Delegate and postpone everywhere. The question I ask if I see someone flatlining is, "What *must* be done this week, such that you will jeopardize the welfare of the

organization if you do not attend to it?" If you were sick
for a week, what would you outsource and what would be
postponed? We all know what we *want* to accomplish in
a week, but when you learn to operate on two lists—the
nonnegotiables and the wishes—you can quickly adjust the
plan when you feel yourself burning out.

9. **Put refueling activities in the calendar first.** You will
    never be caught up. You will never have time. If you are a
    high achiever, especially if you are an owner or executive,
    you will always have tension between what you want to
    achieve and the time available. Put the refueling activities
    and vacations on the calendar first and then plan around
    them.

10. **The process doesn't stop, but you will get better at
    managing it.** When you focus on fuels, drains, and buffers,
    you'll begin recognizing little warning signs that you are
    running thin. You'll get better at refueling earlier and
    bouncing back more quickly.

Finally, we need to have an answer when we ask ourselves, "Why
am I doing this?" If we run an organization, why are we doing it? If
we lead, what do we want to achieve? If we are building businesses
or innovating systems, what is our end goal? What do you want to
be proud of when you die?

We can sustain activity for a limited time without having a deeper
purpose. Eventually, goals that feel meaningless or contradict our

values will create a feeling of lethargy. This sense of ennui becomes an additional energy drain because we do not feel like ourselves. By contrast, connecting with the purpose of what we do helps us to cope with the daily drains and allows us to refuel more quickly. (Go to https://www.relationalgenius.com for additional resources on burnout.)

KEY TAKEAWAYS

1. *When you give more than feels comfortable, you increase the chances that resentment will occur.*

2. *Managing your emotional vomit will help those around you.*

3. *If you are easily affected (or infected) by emotional vomit, proactively protect yourself and create distance from the perpetrators.*

4. *Energy is finite. Sharpen your awareness of what fuels you and what drains you to prevent burnout.*

LEADERSHIP APPLICATION

1. If you are in a leadership position, you can't afford to resent the people depending on you. It will lower morale and create toxicity. Keep firm boundaries to protect relationships.

2. If you want to lead with sustainable excellence, you must prioritize refueling activities. As a leader, there will never be a time when you are "caught up." Practice the self-discipline of prioritizing yourself.

Part I focused on the elements of you—the personal sphere of self-knowledge and emotion that also impacts other people. Part II adds a layer: how you intersect with other people. When you show confidence, teach people how to treat you, and make wise decisions about whom to trust, others will take you seriously.

Part II

—

GETTING PEOPLE TO TAKE YOU SERIOUSLY

Chapter 5

CONFIDENCE

When I reached out to a few of my clients about this book's title, two of my most successful clients adamantly pushed for an option with the word "confidence" in it. One said, "I think the people who care about leading a positive personal and professional life often wonder if the things they are doing are the right things."

Increasing our confidence helps with our peace of mind, and it also allows others to take us seriously. It's easier to have confidence in our technical skillsets because the answers are black and white. Further, talking about problems with personal and soft-skill confidence makes us feel vulnerable.

One of my clients, an executive who transitioned to a new company, noted that he was exhausted by meeting many new people. He wondered if it was normal. I assured him that it was and said,

"You're taking in the logistical information, figuring out who they are, and simultaneously asking the question that none of us are supposed to have: 'Do they like me?'"

In my experience, high achievers' self-worth and performance are not linearly correlated. (If you hated statistics class, that means that your confidence does not increase as your performance increases.) As I mentioned in chapter 1, it is normal for high achievers to be at the top of their game and still ask, "Am I enough?"

> *"I have this duality, in which I know that I objectively perform at a higher level than everyone else, but I simultaneously have a lot of self-doubts."*
>
> —From the high achievers who are most likely to be voted "Smartest Person in the Room"

THE DISCREPANCY BETWEEN PERSONAL AND TECHNICAL CONFIDENCE

Many high achievers struggle with self-doubt because they have a discrepancy between their personal and technical confidence. First, if you don't struggle with personal confidence, you might want to skim this section. I haven't surveyed all high achievers, so I don't know for a fact that everyone experiences this discrepancy. I have answered many questions about the disparity, so I want to explain it here.

The high achiever pattern that I observe mirrors the work of Alfred Adler, a psychologist who coined the term "inferiority complex." Adler theorized that many of us encounter some type of deficiency when we are young, which engenders feelings of inferiority.

Sometimes the feeling about a real or perceived deficit generalizes such that we feel "less than" other people. We make ourselves feel better about the deficiency by excelling in other areas. These efforts are called compensatory strivings. Compensatory strivings develop into a drive to be superior. Here is the practical application of the theory.

Sometimes parents, peers, or others make comments when we are young that wound us. The statements make us feel inferior about our appearance, personality, or people skills. Yet the infection often spreads and downgrades our overall sense of value. Many of the wounds are lies, based on other people's insecurities and biases. Yet we take them as truth and see ourselves accordingly.

Do I believe that all high achievers pursued achievement to compensate for inferiority? Not necessarily. The approval for high achievement is addictive, and if we receive praise for our successes, our brains can quickly conflate achievement with personal value. Some families celebrate first-place trophies and throw away the second-place ones. The As get ice cream; the Bs get a lecture. If we don't simultaneously learn that we are unique and special apart from our performance, our confidence will suffer in any situation where we feel second-place.

Sometimes we manage to make it through childhood and young adulthood unscathed. Later, a toxic personal or work relationship causes us to doubt ourselves and our judgment. If you are in a relationship with a romantic partner or a boss who undermines you, you may experience a slow erosion of personal confidence.

When we doubt our worth, we compensate by working hard to be "good enough." Thus, our confidence is always vulnerable to our momentary wins or lapses. We continuously strive to prove our worth. This striving forms the foundation for the duality in which high achievers know that they objectively perform at a higher level than everyone else, but they simultaneously doubt themselves. When we conflate performance with personal value, we will always wonder if we are measuring up.

Low confidence in our value reduces our ability to interact optimally with others. We may be less likely to set boundaries, join conversations, or make unpopular decisions. Alternately, we may embrace being different than others but secretly want others to approve of us. Beyond the stress to our social interactions, low confidence creates a massive energy drain because of our internalized pressure to perform and the negative self-talk that occurs if we fail.

High achiever argument: "But if low confidence made me work hard, won't self-acceptance cause me to lose my motivation for excellence?"

Here's my answer. Most high achievers have been striving for excellence for a long time. When did you start wanting praise? When did your focus on being "at the top" begin? When we have strived for 10, 20, or 30 years to be the best, we develop neurological and behavior patterns that become a default. Changing our defaults takes intentional, sustained effort. If you think about the work you've done to alter a bad habit, you'll understand the degree to which your attention to excellence is unlikely to spontaneously disappear.

I'm not asking you to settle for being mediocre, because I don't think you could do that, even if you tried. I am asking you to challenge your perception of a linear correlation between personal value and peak performance. I want you to acknowledge your worth, even if you make mistakes or fail. **If we take responsibility for low performance while retaining personal confidence, we expend less energy on masking, accommodating, or overcoming our insecurities. We can tolerate feedback and failure without being crushed.**

Personal confidence encompasses not only our strengths but also our weaknesses. When we can make a list of our shortcomings and then say, "I'm still a great person, and I respect myself," we automatically begin teaching other people how to treat us. Personal confidence allows us to move in a way that automatically yields more influence. We can be kind without fear of being a doormat. We can apologize for our mistakes without apologizing for ourselves. We can use our voice and know that it matters, even if not everyone agrees. We don't feel the compulsion to engage in power struggles, because we have nothing to prove. We can freely admit weaknesses without being unduly embarrassed because we know that our imperfections do not define us. The people around us sense this core confidence and automatically are less likely to mistreat or take advantage of us.

Fun fact: Even if you struggle with confidence, confidently acknowledging your difficulties with confidence makes you appear more confident.

HOW TO SHOW CONFIDENCE WHEN YOU FEEL INSECURE

If your confidence helps people take you seriously, what do you do when you feel insecure? Most people, even with high confidence, struggle with some insecurity. We appear more confident and have more power when we simply acknowledge a specific insecurity instead of attempting to mask it. If we are insecure about something, someone will eventually hit that button, and we will experience strong emotional reactions. Alternatively, we might close down emotionally and push people away. As I've mentioned before, people's assumptions and conclusions are usually more damaging than the truth. A simple script to use when someone hits your insecurity button is:

> **Script:** "I feel a little vulnerable in this area; could you please give me some time to process it?"

Most people will instantly understand and give you time or try to make you feel emotionally safe. While calling out your insecurity makes you feel vulnerable, the result will be better than attempting to disguise it.

Difficult People Warning: *Never* acknowledge insecurity issues with a toxic person (more information in Part IV: Toxic Games). Toxic people will use the knowledge to manipulate you.

QUESTIONS AND TIPS TO BUILD YOUR CONFIDENCE

1. What are some of the lies or fallacies that you have believed about yourself? Take time to learn where these beliefs originated.

2.   If you are in an organization that values confidence more than authenticity, work with someone safe to help you "fake" the confidence while you are building it.

3.   In interviews of any kind, don't try to be good enough. People can smell desperation. Instead, figure out your strengths and what you have to offer. Trust that if it's the right fit, people will see those strengths. This approach removes the pressure of trying to prove yourself, and you will come across as competent and confident.

4.   *Do not make assumptions* about what other people are thinking of you. It is a confidence killer, and you are usually wrong.

TAKING COMPLIMENTS – A "TELL" FOR INSECURITY OR CONFIDENCE

The ability to take compliments reveals confidence; it is a behavior that helps people to take us seriously. When you don't take compliments, you appear insecure. You may also be emotionally exhausting, inadvertently insulting, and sometimes hurtful. These outcomes reduce interpersonal power.

- **Emotionally exhausting:** When people give compliments to be nice to you, arguing the compliment costs *them* energy.

- **Insulting:** Dismissing people's compliments can make them feel like you don't value their judgment.

- **Hurtful:** When someone genuinely cares, dismissing their compliments can feel like a slap in the face. Giving heartfelt compliments can make people feel vulnerable, and they may feel criticized or dumb when you push them away.

- **Strategically dumb:** *Exhibit A:* You want your life to be full of people who genuinely care about you, have your back, and will go to bat for you, right? Yet you alienate these very people when you push away their compliments.

  Exhibit B: If you cannot graciously acknowledge compliments in professional situations, you show that you are insecure. At best, this creates doubt about your confidence and leadership abilities. At its worst, it makes you a target for toxic people who will pick up on the insecurity and use it against you.

Benefits of taking a compliment: It makes the other person feel good. I sent a quick email to one of my clients one day. *Hey, I forget to tell people sometimes how much I appreciate them. I love having you as my client.* The client's reply: *Thanks! I love having you as my coach!* It was such a simple exchange, and it made me smile. Thanking someone for a compliment acknowledges the gift they are trying to give you. Accepting a compliment also shows that you have self-esteem, which, in turn, gains more respect from others and helps them to take you seriously.

Feeling and showing confidence is one of the first steps in getting people to take us seriously. We need to value and respect ourselves before we can expect anyone else to do the same. Confidence also provides the strength to implement the next chapter's strategies on teaching people how to treat you.

KEY TAKEAWAYS

1. *Confidence in your personal value differs from confidence in your performance.*

2. *High achievement will never substitute for the core confidence that you are loved, that you are valued, and that you belong.*

3. *Increasing your confidence will not decrease your motivation to excel.*

4. *It's more fun to win (perform) when you love the competition but are not trying to prove your worth.*

LEADERSHIP APPLICATION

1. Leaders who struggle with personal confidence often try to prove themselves through performance. This approach leads to an overemphasis on their skillset as a means for gaining status or respect. Simultaneously, they may distance themselves emotionally to avoid hurt and rejection. Hence, their leadership style minimizes connection and dismisses the power of relationship capital. Leaders who fit into this category often get frustrated when they see less skilled peers "get ahead" in acquiring new opportunities.

2. Confidence in your leadership skills doesn't mean that you know everything. Leading requires dealing with multiple people and an infinite number of changing variables. It's impossible to predict all of the sequences. Instead, focus on your strengths and the core values you cherish as a leader. Seek books, coaches, and mentors to increase your skills, close knowledge gaps, or solve specific scenarios. The best leaders continuously walk into the unknown; therefore, mistakes and new learning are the cost of outstanding leadership.

Chapter 6

TEACHING PEOPLE HOW TO TREAT YOU

O nce personal confidence is established, it is easier to teach people how to treat us. Outworking other people, being the glue that holds everything together, being the kindest person in the room—all of these are valuable, but none of them alone will get people to respect you. In this chapter, you will learn the power of precedent setting, the importance of the messages you send about yourself, and the importance of scarcity. By mastering these soft-skill components and consistently implementing them, you teach people how to treat you.

SETTING PRECEDENTS AND EXPECTATIONS

Precedent setting teaches people how to treat you. Unfortunately, we always set precedents, whether we intend to or not. People's brains quickly develop rules and cognitive shortcuts. Thus, the first few interactions are critical in determining subsequent behavioral pathways. If you do not want to answer emails at 3 a.m., do not respond at 3 a.m. If you do not want people to cancel at the last minute, do not accommodate last-minute schedule changes. If you do not want someone to be offensive, do not laugh when he or she tries to pass off a comment as a joke.

In chapter 4, I explained the resentment risk of making exceptions to one's boundaries. There is also a nonemotional reason to avoid doing so. When we deviate from a pattern, we confuse people's brains. How quickly do you get off course on weeks that have a Monday holiday? Logically, you know the week is different; behaviorally, you find yourself following the wrong day. I've learned that no matter what I *say*, the expectations are set based on what I *do*.

Setting the precedents you want means staying consistent with people until they can understand what constitutes your norms and expectations. If sticking with your preferences is difficult for you, think about what you want long-term. Do you want positive relationships, or do you want broken ones? Do you prefer efficient systems, or do you want inefficient ones? Do you want the freedom to focus, or do you want constant interruptions?

We are most vulnerable to unwittingly setting bad precedents at the early stages of relationships. At a later time, we can make allowances without the same concern of precedent setting. After you set precedents, you can flexibly collaborate with others, and everyone appreciates it. Their brains have encoded the norm, and they understand alternate behavior as an exception.

Here are some common areas where appropriate precedents save energy and promote positive interactions:

- **Phone conversations:** What is the longest phone conversation you want to have? Make a habit of ending the chat 10 minutes before that time. (Ten minutes is arbitrary, but it accommodates the planning fallacy that both of you will speak beyond your cutoff time.)

- **New work environments:** In new professional environments, intentionally vary your rhythm of work time, availability, and email responses to avoid setting precedents. You want to figure out the optimal flow and then set precedents accordingly.

- **Requests:** Across all situations—say "no" more often than you need to in the beginning. This pattern will safeguard against you being perceived as agreeable and available, which will translate to you feeling unappreciated and used six months later.

Mix up the "nos" with strategic "yeses." Occasionally, volunteer to help, especially if you initially say no a lot. You want to send the message that you are a team player, but you are not a "yes man / yes woman."

- **Business procedures:** The extra attention, flexibility, or "one-time" discounts to new customers set precedents. You may want to close a sale or make new customers feel welcome, but they assume that these initial practices represent what they can expect in the future. Remember that precedents are set according to behavior rather than words. Verbal or written explanations that this is a one-time event will not change their emotional expectations.

Changing a precedent

If you have inadvertently set a precedent, here is your script:

Script: "I'm sorry. I believe that I sent mixed messages. I'm not available to work after ___ time, so I'll wrap up meetings before then. I wanted to give you a heads-up so that I don't confuse you."

Then, change your behavior accordingly. You *must* be consistent after you recite the script. If you make allowances, you make the situation worse by adding a bad precedent...that people shouldn't take you seriously when you set a boundary.

VERBAL-NONVERBAL CONGRUENCE

Just as behavioral consistency supports verbal precedents, our nonverbals add or detract from our message. Our facial expressions and tone of voice must align with our statements. When I first began speaking up for my needs, I was confused and angry when people didn't take me seriously. Finally, I asked someone why my message got lost. She said, "I heard you say it, but you were smiling the whole time, so I didn't think you were that serious about it." I intended to take the edge off of the conflict. The smile gave a different impression—that I wasn't serious. My words were exact, but people were acting on my nonverbals.

When you want people to hear you, have full, straight-on eye contact, use a serious tone of voice, and keep a straight face. In high-stakes situations, you can exert power by extending eye contact and slowing your speech rate. Never, ever make threats unless you fully intend to follow through. If your behavior and your facial expressions are consistent, people will take you seriously. You won't have to repeat yourself, because people will hear you the first time. Whenever I role-play this strategy with clients, their response is, "Wow, you are scary." Full-on eye contact with a straight face sends a message that you are implacably standing your ground.

VISUAL CUES

In addition to facial cues, our brains process other visual cues when we assess people. Someone's walk, speech, appearance, or environmental cues (offices, cars) give information about confidence, power, socioeconomic status, and mental frame of mind.

My brain is especially tuned in to walk and posture. People who walk with their shoulders slumped and their eyes downcast send an instant message that they lack confidence. At best, they look like a nonentity; at worst, they are an easy target for unscrupulous people.

Some people are very aware of others' environments. I have often heard people describe someone's office or desk when they discuss the person. "She was nice enough but seemed disorganized. Her office is a wreck." Our brains use cognitive shortcuts to deal with the massive amounts of information coming our way, and whether we like it or not, visual information is part of that process.

The good news is that you don't have to have a perfect presentation to be taken seriously. People will forgive the messy office if you have a confident and neat personal presentation. Suppose you are in a wheelchair or have a muscular difficulty that adversely affects your posture; you can command attention and respect through eye contact or clothing choices. I prefer leopard-print dresses over power suits, so I display my credentials and awards on my office wall.

I encourage you to look at all of the different variables and then choose a combination that allows you to feel like yourself. **The most potent factor, the quiet core confidence that you deserve to be taken seriously, will override all visual cues.**

SCARCITY

Monitoring our precedents and presentation helps people to take us seriously. Scarcity also increases perceived value. Let's suppose that you love yellow roses. You go to a market and see a stand overflowing with them. There is only one pink rose in the middle. Even though you came for the yellow roses, what draws your eye? Maybe you walk quickly to grab it before someone else has the opportunity.

Alternately, you have reached your favorite restaurant, and you notice that a different restaurant close by has a line of people outside. Will you take note and go back to that restaurant next week? When we perceive something as scarce, we value it more highly, sometimes even more so than the object of our original preference. *(The principle of scarcity is the psychology behind all of those time-limited offerings in sales.)*

People who are always available, always ready to help, always forgiving, and always unassuming—regardless of how they are treated—will always be undervalued. They will be appreciated but never prioritized because no one has to do any work to maintain the relationship. Hence, they are left to wonder why everyone else gets ahead. Do we value air? Absolutely. We freak out when we can't breathe. But do we walk around being grateful for air? Of course not. We assume it will always be there.

People who are eager to please will be undervalued if they work to get others' approval at all costs. In an odd twist of humanity, we all value a tiny bit of emotional scarcity. People sense when we are kind from a place of confidence or from a position of needing approval. They can "smell it" if we're impressive due to our standards or because we are trying to impress them. **If people believe that you need them more than they need you, you will never be scarce enough to be appreciated.**

You can be generous and still "scarce." If you set appropriate precedents and maintain healthy boundaries, people appreciate your availability instead of taking it for granted. I provide concierge services, which means that I am available to my clients between appointments. Business advisors and friends have asked me about the limits I place on the interactions so that people don't take advantage of me. It has never been a problem. In fact, I am dedicated to going "above and beyond" for them. One might think that I am violating the principle of scarcity, but I never feel used. They respect me, and they never take advantage of me. Why?

1. I screen potential clients, and the people I accept have good boundaries.

2. I work with high achievers, who hate asking for help in the first place.

3. I expect them to work hard; I am not "easy."

4. I would fire someone if he or she tried to take advantage of me.

(Shout-out to my clients—thank you.)

INFLUENTIAL POWER

Influence is a step above being taken seriously. When people take you seriously, they respect you. When people see you as someone with influence, they allow you to impact their lives. If you have influential power, people will voluntarily follow you. Positional power (i.e., a higher title) may accompany influential power, but this is not always the case. Many people hold positions of power, but they have no influence.

Giving Power to Get Power

If you want influential power, give power instead of fighting to keep it. When we voluntarily give away power, we automatically send a message that we can share power without feeling threatened. If you witness people being generous with money, you probably assume they have a lot of it, right? If you notice people being generous with food, you probably believe there is plenty.

If you witness a confident and successful person being generous with power, what do you assume? When you have personal power, you do not need to argue minor details. You do not need to engage in one-upmanship to prove your worth. You prefer to put your energy into a more significant agenda, which, in turn, buys you more power.

There is one caveat. I included "confident" and "successful" in the paragraph above. Giving away power only works when we are scarce enough to be taken seriously. If you lack self-esteem and attempt to get approval by being agreeable, you cannot use this tactic yet. People will not view you as someone with power; they will assume that you are a pushover. I know that might be frustrating, but work on building your self-esteem first.

How to Lose Influence—the Cost of Being Right

Sometimes people mistake being right for being powerful. If you need to be right to feel validated, you lose influential power. People can see your lack of personal confidence if you are adamant about your "rightness'" without acknowledging a different perspective.

Some analytical high achievers, governed by a high value of logic and fairness, prefer to argue a point into the ground. It's not that they have a personal need for validation; they demand accuracy, and they want to make the other person see things correctly. The problem with the pursuit of agreement to win an argument is that you jeopardize the relationship and lose influence. Sometimes people will agree just to make you shut up and go away.

I remember the year that I decided I didn't need to be right. I felt the change first—that being wrong about something wasn't indicative of personal failure. Thus, I started saying, even when I was confident, "I don't have to be right about this." If I was wrong, I quickly acknowledged it: "You are right, and I am wrong." My nonverbals show confidence, so people don't misinterpret the statements as derivative of low self-esteem. I remember the freedom that came with those words. I no longer felt pressured to make an argument or have someone agree with me.

Here are some examples of the way people lose influence when they value rightness over relationship:

1. Two department heads in a healthcare organization are at war. One goes out of his way to expose the other person as wrong. By doing so, he puts his insecurity on display for everyone else to see, thus lowering his status.

2. Someone receives a positive performance review. There are two inaccuracies, and the person belabors these points for an hour, asking the reviewer to provide supporting evidence of them.

3. In a public situation, someone argues another person's viewpoint. The longer the argument, the higher the relational cost. On the other hand, graciously

acknowledging the different perspectives and agreeing to disagree allows both people to win.

Script: "I need to retain my position, but you make some good points. I do understand your view and the reasons you are so passionate about it."

Teaching others how to treat us lessens the drama. We don't have to repeat ourselves as often, and we don't make other people's bad behavior into our emergencies. The boundaries that arise from setting and maintaining the expectations about what we will allow into our environment give us the space to focus on essential priorities and increase our influence. The process of teaching people how to treat us is much easier when we make wise decisions about whom to trust in the first place. The next chapter will help you make choices about the people who will most likely treat you well.

KEY TAKEAWAYS

1. *No one will take you seriously if you don't take yourself seriously.*

2. *Whatever is easily accessible is also quickly taken for granted.*

3. *If you engage in a pointless competition to prove your superiority, everyone will see your insecurity.*

LEADERSHIP APPLICATION

1. As your leadership influence broadens, you will receive an ever-increasing number of requests. If you have a kind and generous spirit, you will want to respond to more people than you should and feel guilty if you do not. Your availability will continue to change as your organization grows. Figure out ways of being caring and accessible, but set parameters and be consistent with them. Otherwise, your teams and your organization will suffer from your lack of focused attention.

2. If you need to reprimand a subordinate, make sure your face and tone reflect the matter's seriousness. Have a sit-down, eye-to-eye-contact discussion. If you mention it in passing or state the problem lightly, the subordinate will underestimate the matter's severity. Later, you will feel frustrated at the unresolved issue.

3. If you are in a politically charged atmosphere in which there is a power competition, do not engage in open debate to prove a point. If you get in the mud, the mud will get on you. Instead, pull back, gather information, seek counsel, and develop a more strategic approach.

Chapter 7

CHOOSING THE PEOPLE WHO WILL TREAT YOU WELL

"I don't always trust my judgment about people. What if I'm wrong?"

—From a business partner who trusted
too easily and landed in a legal battle

ncreasing our confidence and teaching people how to treat us helps everyone take us more seriously. When you increase your effectiveness of choosing whom to trust and how they fit into your life, you will surround yourself with people who respect your boundaries and take you seriously. In this chapter, you will learn specific indicators and red flags related to trust. From there, you will learn how to determine the relationship level of people in your life.

HOW DO I KNOW WHOM TO TRUST?

Trusting too quickly and not trusting at all are equally problematic. When we assume the best and ignore red flags, we make ourselves or our businesses vulnerable. If we decide not to trust at all, we isolate ourselves from moral support, information, and opportunity. Over the years, I have witnessed the degree to which relationships are the foundations of happiness. Stress, fulfillment, success, purpose—whatever topics we discuss, we end up circling back to relationships. It is impossible to live fully without taking a chance on relationships. But how do you take a calculated risk instead of being all in or all out at the first meeting?

Risking Trust

If you are wary of people because people have hurt you, I want to speak personally to you for a moment. I automatically trusted people until I was in elementary school. At that point, many of my classmates made fun of me for being overweight. Some people didn't tease me, but they excluded me socially. The experience got much worse in junior high school. A good day was a day in which no one made fun of me. The experience taught me to be scared of people—to fear that saying hello would lead to humiliation or rejection. I honestly don't remember how I worked through it, but at some point, I recall thinking, "I need to say hi. Worst-case scenario, this person rejects me. Best-case scenario, I make a friend." I gradually increased my social group, but I still didn't "let people in."

During my master's degree program, I had an epiphany that caused me to seek out one of my professors. In the conversation that ensued, we discussed trust. "Tricia," he said, "you don't have to open the gates all at once. You can open up little by little and see if people are trustworthy. Be a little bit vulnerable; see how people react. If they behave well, open up a little more."

Some of the specific flags on trust combine my psychological expertise with what I learned as I rebuilt my faith in people. There is a hidden set of hoops that people need to jump through to get into my inner circle, and I'm sharing as best I can that information with you. If this sounds like work, it is. The upside is that, one day, you wake up and find yourself surrounded by amazing people. I would not have the close friendships and the impressive clientele that I have today if I hadn't begun taking a chance on trusting people.

Defining "Trustworthy"

Here are the characteristics of the people who have earned my trust:

1. They mean what they say.

2. They will keep my information confidential.

3. They do the right thing, even if it is uncomfortable.

4. They operate by a code of conduct that isn't contingent on popular opinion.

5. They engage in conflict with thoughtfulness and grace.

6. They don't jump to conclusions.

7. I feel safe to be myself.

Your list of attributes for a trustworthy person may be different than mine. It is worth your time to figure out the characteristics of people who have earned your trust. With this information, you can create a template for assessing new relationships.

Below is a list of red flags that reveal a person's lack of trustworthiness. Many people have one or two red flags. You may still keep them in your network; simply adjust your expectations accordingly. After the red flags list, I include a list of indicators (green flags) to help you figure out whom to trust.

Red Flags That Someone May Not Be Completely Trustworthy

1. They gossip, make judgments, or say bad things about other people.

2. They alter their perspective according to their audience.

3. Their behavior does not align with their words.

4. You catch them in small lies that seem inconsequential.

5. They are emotionally impulsive.

6. They emphasize their need for honesty.

7. They take the easy way out on issues of integrity.

Green Flags That Someone Is Stable and Trustworthy

1. If a group of people criticizes a person who is not present, trustworthy people often support the absent person or offer an objective perspective. They do not initiate criticism.

2. They are thoughtful and circumspect. You know that if they have a strong opinion, they can back it up with information *or* they are quick to own it as merely an opinion.

3. They take responsibility and apologize for a misstep. They will own their part in a problem rather than blaming someone else.

4. You notice that they are trusted, liked, and respected by everyone else.

5. They do not like conflict, but they will engage it when necessary. You can depend on them to come to you first if there is a problem.

6. They will say difficult things. Hopefully, they will be kind and gracious in doing so, but you can depend on them for a "real" answer in both business and personal relationships.

7. They are consistent. You know what you're going to get on any given day. Relatedly, their emotional responses are commensurate to the situation. They may get angry or frustrated, but the emotions are congruent to context.

8. They try to give people "the benefit of the doubt" where possible. They are tolerant of other people's idiosyncrasies, but they are not pushovers.

When you try to figure out whom to trust, watch for the people who will be a calm, dissenting voice amid groupthink. These people aren't being a squeaky wheel, argumentative, or trying to play devil's advocate; instead, they value authenticity over comfort. They want to problem-solve, root for the underdog, or offer a different perspective.

If someone stands up for another person, especially if a person in power is doing the critique, he or she will likely stand up for you as well. Group consensus is a powerful social norm. The person who has the strength and integrity to challenge it will be the person who will stand behind you and stand up for you, even when it is not popular. This person garners loyalty and respect from others. He or she is someone you can trust.

The Power of Time in Deciding Whom to Trust

Like many people, I'm attracted to charismatic individuals (hence the adjective, right?). I've often noticed that I connect instantly to the charismatic person in the group, but I build a long-term relationship with one of the less sparkly people. I believe that charismatic people can also have character; however, I've learned to look for a solid foundation beneath the sparkle. If you watch and listen long enough, people will show you everything you need to know.

Whenever you find yourself quick to connect to someone— whether it is because of their personality, their appearance, or shared interest—wait long enough so that you can know them. When I have this discussion with my clients, they inevitably say, "Oh, so it's like dating." Exactly. When you date, the purpose is to see if the initial interest has staying power. You know that spending time in different situations will help you to figure it out. You may need to have many first dates to find the person with whom you want to engage in a long-term relationship. Both business relationships and personal friendships need to carry the same screening process—"I like you. I'm getting to know you. I don't have enough information to marry you."

The Higher the Stakes, the Longer the Wait

Several of my clients have seen me have mini–heart attacks if I think they are trusting too fast in high-stakes business situations. When people see an opportunity that may be mutually beneficial, they get excited and want to rush ahead. This vulnerability paves the way for horrible business partnerships and disappointing hires. Rather than race ahead, slow down the process so that you can spot and adjust for any problematic human factors.

Remember that the execution and sustainability of any positive opportunity rely on the humans who are behind it. Thus, initially slowing down to ensure the character, reliability, and alignment of others will later help you speed up because the foundation is already in place. You also avoid the costs and delays from having to "start over" with someone else. When it comes to stakes, the higher you go, the slower you go.

The Protective Power of Other People

Even if we excel at discerning whom to trust, integrating other people into our decision-making provides a better outcome. They may increase our confidence when their observations align with ours, or they may have insights that protect us from our blind spots.

To See the Things You Do Not See

Despite my best attempts to give you as many concrete signs as possible, some of the markers for trustworthy / not trustworthy people are nebulous. Sometimes we only know that someone's response is unusual. Let me give you an example.

One time, a friend of mine showed me a note from an admirer with whom she felt uncomfortable. She wanted to know if he was merely weird or if he posed a threat. I read the message and said, "Not normal, but harmless." She asked how I knew that from reading the note, and I couldn't give a concise answer. I used my knowledge of psychology and the range of normal behavior to notice cues in terms of sentence structure, word choice, and letter spacing.

The problem with the above example is that I have a natural skillset and specialized knowledge to see those cues. So how do you know what you don't know? I suggest that you rely on the people in your midst who are very good at picking up nuances and intentions in others. There are times when I have not seen a warning flag, but someone else has. Because I took his or her perceptions seriously, I slowed down my decision-making process. Our brains process information so rapidly that people may not always be able to tell you the reason that they distrust someone. They may say, "I have a gut feeling" or "There's something off." Sometimes logical people are quick to discount those explanations because they do not seem factual or evidential.

If you believe that "gut feelings" are woo-hoo, I highly recommend that you read the books called *Blink*, by Malcolm Gladwell, and *The Gift of Fear*, by Gavin de Becker. They provide concrete examples of scenarios in which a "gut feeling" was the brain's rapid processing of the perceptual cues beyond one's awareness. Most of my clients have heard me say, "This is the answer, but I can't tell you why yet. I'll figure it out on the way home." All of the information coalesces into an instinctive answer, but it takes me time to discern the specific clues that led me to a conclusion.

One of my friends has the gift of quickly assessing someone's character. She was frustrated because the other people on a hiring committee dismissed her concerns and chose candidates based on résumé qualifications. Yet the candidates of concern were always bad hires. I called her up as I wrote this and asked, "Did it ever change? Was there a point when the hiring committee took your concerns as the red flags they were?" She told me that they later adopted a hiring procedure where the committee honored any member's concern, regardless of the reason. My friend noted, "It took the pressure off of me because any of us could have that hard-to-explain concern."

To Compare Data

There is no faster way to see a red flag than to have two people compare notes, especially if they meet someone separately. I was screening potential employees for one of my clients. At some point, I asked the candidate what he valued in an employer. He replied, "Honesty." It was an unusual response, and none of the previous information indicated that he had worked in a situation where the employer had been dishonest. When I called my client, I said, "Look, in my experience, the people who talk at length about how they want people to be honest with them are the people who lie the most." My client and I compared notes, and the candidate was lying.

Even when people think that they are keeping the story straight, they respond based on the other person's questions. Business deals and interview situations will benefit from distributed meetings and interviews. Separate one-on-one meetings make people feel more comfortable, and they are more likely to let down their guard or make a mistake in their story.

To Protect Us from Our Ourselves

I have witnessed bad personal or business relationship stories that went like this:

"Everyone told me that he wasn't the right person, but I wouldn't listen. I thought I knew better or that I could make it work."

After listening to enough of these stories, I decided that my friends' and advisors' collective opinion will weigh more heavily than my own. It was a tough decision, as I do not give away power easily. Yet the people in my life are stable, rational, insightful, and not quick to jump to conclusions. Hence, if six people with different backgrounds and specialty areas all see something that I don't, I need to assume that my vision is clouded.

Even if you are a high achiever, you are still vulnerable to the same human pitfalls as everyone else (bummer, right?). We all tend to protect a high emotional investment, even if it yields diminishing returns. We may take shortcuts on due diligence if we see an exciting opportunity. If you can tap into the wisdom of those around you, you can cut your losses earlier in the game. Several of my business-owner clients have a team of advisors. In critical business decisions, if the lawyer, the accountant, and the psychologist all have concerns, the clients integrate that information into their decision-making.

If you have learned not to trust people, and you do not have the close relationships that allow protective feedback, look for a good counselor or coach while you build your support system. I suggest getting one who will give you direct feedback about the people in your life and teach you how to navigate them.

HOW TO MAINTAIN TRUST WITH TRUSTWORTHY PEOPLE

Honesty is the currency that maintains trust in relationships. Of course we want to pay attention to how we deliver the message and how the other person might receive it. However, the truth may sometimes hurt or disappoint the other person.

One of my clients had a tough conversation on his plate. It was going to hurt someone's feelings and possibly create a mess. Ego, power, and money were all part of the conversation. My client described possible approaches that might yield the desired outcome without revealing his real position to others. The other people involved in the client's situation were trustworthy, and the ultimate goal was to maintain the relationships.

While I am a fan of holding one's cards close if people are unknown entities or toxic individuals, that same lack of transparency can hurt high-trust relationships. If telling the truth implodes a relationship, it will implode eventually anyway. The only difference is the amount of time, emotion, and money you lose in the interim. On the other hand, telling the truth from a place of vulnerability and compassion can increase trust, even if the truth isn't pleasant. When we obscure our thoughts and position, we jeopardize the relationship.

After our conversation, I sent this email:

Dear John,

I was thinking about the upcoming conversation with Jack, and I wanted to give you some encouragement on it...specifically about speaking truth on both facts and emotions. There are times when I tell clients to "hold their cards close." In this case, Jack has proved his integrity and has earned the right to transparency.

A lot of people try to gloss over their own emotions and motives in tough situations. This is a huge mistake. People respond to honesty better than a litany of facts. If we try to hide what we think, most people will see right through to our real motives anyway. Other people sense that something is missing, but they don't know what it is. Either way, masking our feelings and intentions erodes trust. They will then second-guess anything we say in the future.

When we put everything on the table, it will be messier at first. Yet when people feel that the conversation is honest, they are much more likely to stay in the game. Long-term, it adds to a reputation of integrity—which increases the speed of trust in future interactions.

I understand how easy it is to want to minimize the potential for conflict, especially for crucial relationships. In my experience, when I avoided conflict, I prolonged the pain. Even when the results were okay, they would have been so much better if I had said, "This is hard for me to say. I need to say it because I've promised that I would always be honest with you."

One of my mentors was the most highly respected and feared person I've met. She had a reputation for tolerating no excuses and making things happen. At a party in honor of her, people stood, and one by one, with no advance coordination, talked about difficult situations—when she told them to "do the right thing." It stayed with me and helped me say the words I don't want to say, do what I don't want to do, and take responsibility that I don't want to take. It never feels great at the moment, but it sure does minimize regrets.

I believe in you.

Tricia

 Difficult People Warning: Do not be transparent with Difficult People, as discussed in Part IV. They will use the information against you.

RELATIONSHIP CATEGORIZATIONS AND EXPECTATIONS

The degree to which we trust others is a significant component of the relationship. We can categorize relationships based on trust levels, shared values, similar interests, or shared worldviews. Observing the degree to which we align with others helps us to have appropriate expectations for the relationship. We can place personal and professional associations somewhere in this diagram of concentric circles.

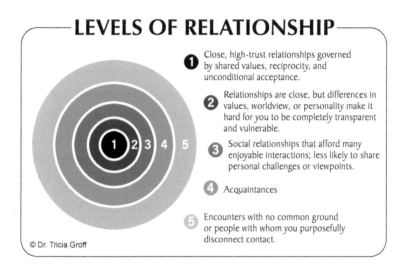

LEVELS OF RELATIONSHIP

1 — Close, high-trust relationships governed by shared values, reciprocity, and unconditional acceptance.

2 — Relationships are close, but differences in values, worldview, or personality make it hard for you to be completely transparent and vulnerable.

3 — Social relationships that afford many enjoyable interactions; less likely to share personal challenges or viewpoints.

4 — Acquaintances

5 — Encounters with no common ground or people with whom you purposefully disconnect contact.

© Dr. Tricia Groff

There is nothing intrinsically right or wrong about these levels. When we know the characteristics of each category, we can place people accordingly and maintain appropriate expectations. We don't need everyone to be our best friend; on the other hand, it's good to invest effort into the people who might make it into that circle.

Performance-Based Expectations

When you assess whether someone will be a trusted confidante, a good friend, a social partner, or an acquaintance, base your expectations on the facts and behavior at hand. One of my friends told me about a recent friendship with a woman who had no close friends; my friend felt honored that she trusted her. Later, the woman broke the friendship based on an insignificant difference. My friend said, "I should not have thought that I was special. If she is this age and without friends, I should have seen it as a possible red flag."

Use this exact formula for professional relationships. Pay attention to the pattern instead of the potential. If someone has a history of contentious business partnerships, dig into that. You are not unique. Earlier in my career, I got calls from people who said they had worked with 15 counselors, and no one could help them. I did not take them as clients. I have turned down business partnerships based on poor communication, regardless of goal alignment. If the communication fit is problematic at the onset, I have no reason to expect it to improve.

Know what you need from people at the various levels, and then let the relationship evolve. If you see red flags, it doesn't mean that the person can't be part of your life. Rather, you simply want to adjust your expectations of where they will land in the relationship diagram.

People are who they are, not who we want them to be. You will see this theme repeat itself throughout this book because understanding it is key to being a relational genius. If we can accept people as they are, we can honor what they bring to the table instead of judging them for what they are missing.

KEY TAKEAWAYS

1. Let your observations determine your level of trust.

2. Use trusted friends or advisors to help you assess people when the stakes are high.

3. You can retain relationships with people you don't wholly trust; simply manage your expectations and information disclosure accordingly.

LEADERSHIP APPLICATION

1. If you are considering a business partnership or any relationship in which your success and sanity are contingent on someone else's good behavior, please go to the *www.relationalgenius.com* resource site for more information.

2. Do not disclose sensitive information in professional environments until you learn who keeps information confidential.

3. If you break trust, be up-front and honest to preserve and rebuild the relationship.

4. If you have to choose between maintaining someone's approval or maintaining their trust, choose trust. Approval feels good, but trust gets the job done.

In Parts I and II, we focused on understanding ourselves, interacting effectively with the people in our circle, and making decisions about whom to bring into that circle. Part III will help you read people. When we understand human patterns, we can develop heuristics that allow us to interact effectively, even if we don't have all of the information available.

Part III

UNDERSTANDING AND ASSESSING OTHER PEOPLE

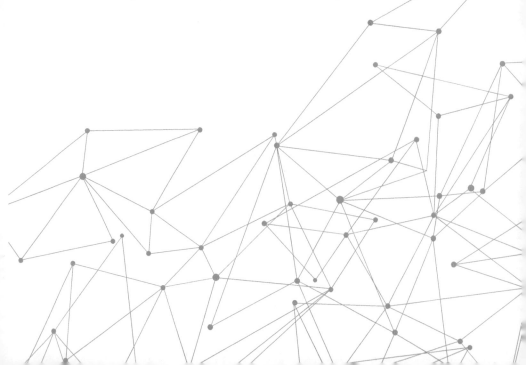

Chapter 8

HUMAN NEEDS– YOU NEED TO KNOW THIS TO BE EFFECTIVE

In this chapter, you will learn how to recognize and respond to human needs. If you familiarize yourself with these needs and assume that everyone has them, you'll be able to respond effectively to a wide variety of people. These needs are like food and water; we all behave better when we have them, and we regress when we don't.

THE NEED FOR FREEDOM AND AUTONOMY

People don't like being told what to do. You already know this, right? They don't like being told what to do, even when you want to help them. The only exception I have found to this rule is when people pay me to tell them what to do. Even then, I use phrases like "This is my suggestion; alter it so it feels like you," and "I feel strongly about this, but I don't have to be right." I want to acknowledge their human need for autonomy.

The first thing that you will want to remember is that all people have some degree of psychological reactance. In psychology, the term "psychological reactance" means our emotional response to anything that seems to limit our freedom. All people will experience some reactance when others tell them what to do, but the reaction is particularly intense for some people.

© Dr. Tricia Groff

In my PhD program, one of my colleagues loved bubble baths. After a particularly grueling day, I said, "Hey, Mike, have a good evening! Be nice to yourself and take a bubble bath." He replied, "Well, Tricia, I was going to, but now that you told me to, I'm not so sure that I will. I don't like to have my freedoms limited." *(I wanted to put that anecdote into a cartoon, but my wiser self realized that a picture of a female in an office setting asking a male if he is going to take a bubble bath might not be the way to go.)*

If you want to experiment with reactance, borrow a teenager. Teenagers, who are all discovering their identity, hate outside pressure. Hence, parents who give lectures get the opposite behavior of what they want. When I worked with teenagers, I had a strategy to get them to trust me. In our first appointment, I said, "Are you here because you want to be here or because your parents brought you? If you were forced here, I'm sorry. I *hate* when people tell me what to do." The teens leaned forward and shouted, *"Me too!!!!"* as if I'd just announced that we had the same obsession with a specific music group.

Great salespeople are successful because they respect prospects' needs for autonomous decision-making. We run away (well, I do anyway) from the bad salespeople who seem intent on telling us what we should do while disregarding our needs.

One of the phrases I use most often when potential clients contact me about services is "No pressure." I do not like being pressured, so I find it distasteful to pressure others. I also want people to say yes from a place of excitement and commitment.

When you have conversations that value people's freedom of choice, you give them a sense of personal power and ownership over their decisions. Whether you are trying to convince a spouse, a business partner, or an organizational stakeholder, remove the pressure if you want buy-in. The resulting behavior is much more sustainable than if he or she simply succumbed to situational coercion.

THE NEED FOR UNCONDITIONAL ACCEPTANCE

Here is the gooey truth many high achievers don't like to acknowledge: everyone needs to feel love for who they are, not for what they do or what they can give. Everyone needs unconditional acceptance. I know you feel more comfortable focusing on analytics and performance, but integrating this concept can make you a phenomenal leader.

There are a lot of videos that show humans and their pets. Some videos are attention-grabbing because they show bonds between humans and bears, tigers, or other nontraditional pets. Many people like watching the animals. I like to watch the humans.

Grown-ups show all of their emotional needs when they are interacting with their animals. You can see them move in for an animal hug, kiss the animal on the head, or cuddle the animal close. If one were to judge only by appearance, I believe that some of these people would not be caught dead showing the same amount of emotion in any other setting—professionally, personally, or socially. Because animals give love freely, they elicit the amount of safety we need to be vulnerable. In that vulnerability, we can both request love and receive love. (If you don't connect with animals, think about small children. Many of us lower our guard with them as well.)

People often think about love in the context of romantic, family, or friend relationships. Love parses into the yearning for acceptance, the desire to be seen, and the longing to be valued. If we attend to these needs, we hit the gold mine that drives positive human interactions.

Do you have someone in your life who you just *know* thinks that you are the best thing since sliced bread? You know they see you. They know who you are. They know that you are not perfect, yet you feel special in their presence. I bet they have a lot of influence in your life, too, don't they?

Because acknowledging deep-seated, awkward, emotional needs is a messy business, we try to remove this variable, especially from our work relationships. Yet, if you want to have influence, you will work hard to make the people around you feel noticed and accepted. Let me give you some examples of how to do that.

1. After I returned to work from running my first marathon, one of my colleagues presented me with a framed poster of my race statistics. Everyone had signed it with their words of congratulations. I felt seen.

2. I witnessed a moving reaction of someone who received a birthday cake at work. People had not celebrated her in the past, and now she felt she belonged.

3. One of my friends, a VP-level executive, makes a point of greeting each team member in the morning. In turn, the team members feel known.

Early in my career, I decided that people needed to be seen and valued, regardless of their status. My intention was pure, but the worldview benefited me greatly in my academic program and early opportunities. A supervisor at my internship assignment told me about the glowing recommendations I had received. I was flattered but also curious. I had no idea what I was doing "right," so I decided to ask this incredibly awkward question of a trusted professor: "Dr. _____, could you help me understand why you all like me? I mean, I appreciate it, and I think you're great, but there are a lot of other good students. What am I doing that is working?"

She paused and thought about it a second. "You see us as people, not just as professors. You ask us about how our day is going or how we are feeling." Her answer gave me the key to understanding the social currency that drives human decision-making. People want to be seen and valued as people, regardless of their role.

Many of my clients push back at me in our discussions about others' needs for approval and acceptance. "I don't want to brown-nose." "I don't want to be fake." It's not about brownnosing, bull-shitting, or manipulating. Find the points that you can truthfully say that will honor someone. I mentioned this concept at my leadership book club, noting the degree to which people feel like they are fake if they give a compliment to someone they don't like. The person beside me instantly got it. "Come on. There has to be at least one little good thing you can find about someone else, even if it's her little fingernail."

I don't have to approve of the whole person to ask how his or her day is going. I may be around someone who drives me crazy, but I can find a way to be compassionate for her humanity. Sometimes I need help to find compassion. I remember a particularly challenging day early in my career when I had two clients who stretched my patience. They were both lonely, and the loneliness made them misbehave. That said, understanding the source of the behavior didn't diminish the energy drain. On the morning of their appointments, I prayed, "God, can you please help me show compassion instead of judgment?" In the afternoon, both clients brought me flowers. Compassion came pretty easily after that.

Maybe you don't have a particular spiritual orientation, but you have a mantra or a set of value statements that guide you. Alternately, maybe you can run the situation past someone else. Sometimes one of my clients says, "Tricia, I can't tolerate this person. Can you help me figure out how I can feel differently?" The point is that we don't have to automatically feel warm, happy feelings toward people to find the good.

A lot of people try to navigate professional deals based on facts, logic, and interests. These variables are essential, but not the most important. If you can authentically value people, they will feel seen and safe in your presence. This heightened level of trust increases decision-making efficiency. Instead of spending their energy trying to figure out your real motives and intentions, people can simply focus on the decision at hand and ensure that it's a good one.

The Crusty Marshmallows

Some people come across as not needing to be loved by others. They may be aloof, abrasive, or appear unaffected by human interactions. During college, I was scared of statistics class. The concepts made sense to me; the formulas did not. Fortunately, my first statistics professor taught in both words and formulas. I did well in the class, and gradually my confidence rose—that is, until it was time for

Statistics II. The teacher was brusque, and I was scared of him. I wasn't sure how the class would work if I didn't feel comfortable asking for additional explanations as I had done previously.

Knowing that I needed a plan, I voiced my concern to my first professor. He said, "Oh, don't worry about Mr. M. He is like a burnt marshmallow, hard and crusty on the outside...soft and gooey on the inside." From that point on, I acted on the faith that he was a marshmallow. I asked for help, gave him compliments, and entered into his space the same way I had learned to do with other professors. Frankly, I never knew what reached the marshmallow part and what bounced off the crusty exterior, but we got along well, and I succeeded in the class.

I have applied the crusty marshmallow metaphor with all people who appear to be impervious to human emotion. Occasionally, if I feel safe (or sassy) enough, I tell them that I know they are marshmallows. I've called out aggressive litigators and Special Forces.

They look shocked and embarrassed, but the interaction increases their trust in me because I've "seen" them. The reason that reaching for the gooey marshmallow works is that it is a human place that most people do not dare to touch.

Humans tend to take each other at face value. It's easy to assume that people who appear nonemotional are not emotional. Some crusty marshmallows come across as "all business," not showing any indication of a personal side. Some marshmallows act like jerks. I told one of my marshmallows that he is a porcupine marshmallow; he has hard, pointy edges to keep people away. Caring requires looking closely enough to see if there is more than what people first present. Assuming that there is something more and acting on it requires courage. We might be wrong. Maybe there is no gooey softness—just black char and a cutting insult that makes us feel stupid for taking the risk.

I still feel stupid about 75% of the time that I first reach in to touch the marshmallow instead of the crusty exterior. I feel vulnerable. I might give a genuine compliment, ask a personal question, or write a little note. Each time, I understand that if I'm wrong, the gesture may be disregarded, or worse, viewed as silly. Sometimes I get no response or a negative response, and my feelings get hurt. Yet I get just enough feedback to give me the courage to continue. Sometimes I see a note I'd written hanging by someone's desk. Once, I sent a heartfelt email to someone who rarely commented on my communication. I felt vulnerable in trying to be helpful. Several weeks later, he offhandedly mentioned that he had read the email "at least 100 times."

Recently, one of my clients asked me how to cope with a curmudgeonly volunteer in his organization. The client was worried about how the volunteer impacted the culture of the organization. As we talked, my client mentioned the man's background. He had no history of someone loving him. At that moment, I ditched my suggestion related to dealing with Difficult People, and I pushed aside creative ideas on facilitating positive cultural norms. Instead, I said, "Bring him brownies." My client said, "Beer?" Sure, either could work. I told him that we needed to speak to the little boy who needed love, rather than the crusty man in front of us. I *know* this may sound hopelessly cliché and like pop psychology...but it's true, and it works. I have noticed that people will run after love, make excuses for it, make bad decisions for it, and center their lives around it. **In my opinion, the power of giving love, of seeing the value in someone who feels unseen, is one of the largest untapped sources for creating change.**

The next day, my client called. "Tricia, you're not going to believe this. I ran into the volunteer, and we talked for close to an hour. It was the best conversation we have ever had. He was even able to take in some of my suggestions for change without getting defensive."

THE NEED TO BE VALUED FOR OUR CONTRIBUTIONS

In addition to our need for unconditional acceptance, we want others to acknowledge our talents and efforts. It is another facet of being "seen."

People need to know that they matter. If you think this is a "duh" statement, it is. Yet many of us assume that the people we appreciate are aware of our feelings. Managers believe that workers know that they are valued. Families take everyday sacrifices for granted and forget to say, "Thank you."

I focus a lot on problem-solving and optimizing the performance of my clients. Thus, even though my people are already excellent, we focus on how to improve. In that focus on improvement, we must call out the value they bring to the table. I've developed the habit of asking them for their "bragging rights" to achieve this.

Logically, it makes sense for us to look at where they've succeeded in the past week so that we can identify contributing variables and hit "repeat." Emotionally, it makes sense to look at the successes because:

1. I want to celebrate my clients.

2. I want to build their confidence.

3. Sometimes I pound on them for an hour; they deserve at least 5 minutes of kindness.

4. I'm trying to correct a common mistake in high achievers, in which their yardstick measures only "How far do we need to go?" versus "How much have we accomplished?"

The first time, I say, "Okay, tell me your bragging rights. What went well this week? What are you proud of?" They say, "I don't need any compliments. I just need to know what to fix." After six months to a year, they say, "Oh wait, Tricia. I didn't tell you about what I did well this week."

Since people need to feel recognized and valued, I believe that we fill that need when we provide compliments or acknowledgment, such as "I appreciate your hard work." In chapter 5, I explained that you exude confidence when you take compliments, which helps people take you seriously. Giving them is equally important. My analytical, high-achieving clients struggle with giving compliments. They feel more at ease on the logical side of discussions and clumsy when it comes to emotion. Hence, giving compliments is often as painful as receiving them.

Here is a real conversation to illustrate. One of my clients, whom I will call Matt, was talking about his employees.

Tricia: "Do you compliment them? Tell them that you appreciate what they are doing?"

Matt: "No, and I don't want to. It's not necessary. If they are doing their job, and I don't say anything negative to them, then it's obvious that I value them and want them to be there."

Tricia: "Look, I've had people on the employee side of the equation who have told me, 'A simple acknowledgment would be nice. I don't need a raise. I don't need special treatment—just a thank-you and some appreciation for the hard work.' Matt, it's such a small thing that makes a big difference."

Matt and I are equally opinionated, and we pushed hard on each other for a few minutes. Then he said, "Tricia, you don't understand. I just can't carry one more thing around in my head that I'm doing wrong and need to do differently." I instantly softened because I got it. He was juggling multiple stressors, and giving compliments was far outside of his comfort zone.

Compliments felt overwhelming to Matt because they felt mushy, vague, and awkward. Compliments do not need to be that way. They can be simple observations, thank-yous, or even passing on a compliment that someone else said.

> **Script:** "Thank you for the effort you have put into this project. I appreciate your dedication."

> **Script:** "Sally was talking about how impressed she was with your management of that situation. I thought I'd let you know." (I usually get permission from the other person to pass on the compliment. I love this approach because it makes the recipient feel good while also building goodwill and group cohesion.)

> **Script:** "I haven't told you lately how much I respect you. I'm glad that you are in my sphere." (This one may feel intense, but it builds relationships.)

When people feel valued, they will be more likely to hear your feedback and less likely to get defensive. You gain the right to be heard, and your influence expands.

THE NEED FOR EMOTIONAL SAFETY—NONJUDGMENT

Do you have anyone in your life who loves you, but is quick to judge other people? You probably are less likely to be vulnerable with them because you know that they might judge you too. When we feel emotionally safe, we know:

1. People will give us the benefit of the doubt.

2. They will not use our words against us.

3. We are free to be ourselves instead of what someone else wants us to be.

If these conditions are met, we are more likely to share what scares us and what hurts us, as well as the dreams that we hesitate to say out loud.

People who do not trust easily will make sure that you are a safe person before telling you what makes them feel vulnerable. Statements that decrease emotional safety include the following:

"I think you're crazy."
"You're overreacting."
"You're too sensitive."
"How can you be so stupid?"
"That idea is never going to work."
"I don't understand what you're upset about."
"It could be worse."

All of these statements minimize the validity of our emotions and viewpoints. I've frequently heard people make these statements and then wonder why their spouse or business partner holds back information. The answer is simple: it's not safe to be completely honest.

We create emotional safety by:

1. listening without reacting and without judging;

2. sharing our shortcomings so that other people know that we are likely to accept them, even if they have faults; and

3. focusing on prioritizing how people will feel after our interactions, rather than focusing only on getting our points across.

People test emotional safety by giving small pieces of information and assessing our reactions. If they tell us something shocking, and we remain compassionate, they will continue to disclose details. If they hear judgment, they may decide to never "open up" to us again.

THE NEED FOR EMOTIONAL SAFETY – PEACE AND A PREDICTABLE ENVIRONMENT

In addition to needing emotional safety to share ourselves without fear of being judged, we need the security that comes from peaceful relationships and predictable environments. Both conflict and unpredictable environments create anxiety in people, which interferes with optimal communication and productivity.

While we all want peace, people who have grown up with substance-addicted or mentally ill parents benefit greatly from stable and predictable environments. As children, we want to feel secure, but children in chaotic households cannot feel secure. They never know if their parents will be angry or happy. Sometimes they don't know what house they will be living in. They learn to cope with the ongoing ambiguity and threat by watching cues in their environments. This hypervigilance and resulting anxiety lasts well into adulthood. You will not always know about this problem. Some people compress anxiety into a ball and appear outwardly calm and collected.

Until I know people's background, I assume that they may have had chaotic home environments. This assumption causes me to do the following:

1. Maintain awareness of my tone of voice. Loud voices (and I have one) can register as yelling. If people are triggered by yelling, they often shut down and are unable to process information. You may be watching them at a boardroom table and never know that it's happening.

2. Tell people who I am and what to expect.

3. Be responsive. Explain deviations in my actions.

4. Obtain information early about how they prefer feedback.

I can't lose with these strategies, because they satisfy critical safety factors for those with difficult childhoods, while enhancing communication with everyone else. Below are additional reminders for conflict and predictability that will optimize all interactions.

Conflict

I hate conflict. Many articles about conflict teach us to embrace it. We feel like we are supposed to feel better about it. Nobody, unless he is in the Difficult Person category, enjoys conflict. People vary in the degree to which they will approach or avoid conflict. My clients want to offer their viewpoints and enjoy lively intellectual debates. However, I cannot recall a single well-adjusted person who said, "Tricia, I would like to have more conflict in my life."

We know that we prefer peaceful relationships, but sometimes it is easy to forget that other people want them as well. If you can approach areas of disagreement with an attitude of "How can we both win? How do we both get on the same page?" you will instantly align yourself with the other person's emotional need. This dynamic allows the appropriate brainstorming and problem-solving to occur.

When you do have difficult conversations, follow them up as often as possible with positive interactions. This sequence sends the message that you will engage in conflict when necessary but shows that you value the other person and want a warm relationship.

Predictability and Responsiveness

Apart from managing conflict, we also create emotional safety when we establish consistency and predictability. We can do this by telling people what is happening and what to expect. We hate when someone says, "We need to talk," because the ambiguity makes us assume the worst. One of my clients was nervous about an all-staff meeting at the end of the week. He had no idea if it was a general update or a layoff. After five days of waiting, the organization canceled the meeting without explanation. A friend is nervous about preparing for a biopsy because she does not know if the provider's warning about nausea means "slightly queasy" or "vomiting all morning." The more specific we can get about what people can expect, the more emotional security we give them. Even if you don't have all of the answers, let people know that you will communicate as more information arrives.

The need for emotional safety accounts for the distress people feel in organizations with poor communication. People need communication to do their jobs, but also to help them "know what's going on." I've noticed that something as simple as closing the loop on email or text can increase or decrease anxiety. I recently was delinquent in responding to someone I value. She had explained something in an email, and it made perfect sense. I read it and thought, *That makes perfect sense*, but I didn't email the thought back. A few days later, I received a check-in from her: *I'm telling myself this story that you are frustrated with me.* It took a lot of courage and trust for her to check in with me. In many relationships, people simply distance themselves or cope with unnecessary anxiety.

Creating systems of responsiveness and telling people what to expect enhances your reputation with fairly little effort. Not only do they view you as safe, but they will likely think that you are organized, competent, and reliable as well.

Simple Scripts: *If you can't offer predictability:* "Sometimes my schedule is unpredictable and my communication sporadic.

Any lag time is not personal. Feel free to check in with me if I have not responded."

If you need responsiveness: "It helps me when people let me know that they have received my communication. Could you please send me a quick 'thanks' or 'okay', even if you don't immediately have time to address it?"

THE POWER OF MEETING NEEDS – CALLING OUT GREATNESS

When we meet people's emotional needs, we set a platform that allows us to see and develop the very best in them. People trust us and give us the right to help them realize their potential. To me, this is "calling out greatness." Everyone is motivated to be at his best when he or she feels accepted, valued, and safe. Speaking to the gooey part of crunchy marshmallows calls out their generosity, kindness, integrity, and warmth.

Sometimes I see someone with a kernel of talent or strength that others take for granted. Most people are not aware of their potential. If we comment on it, celebrate it, and make them aware of it, we call out greatness. We provide the opportunity for it to grow and to be seen by others as well.

Remember the statistics professor, the one who introduced the crusty marshmallow concept to me? He intentionally called out the greatness in his students. Each semester, he chose a handful of students in whom he saw potential. He wrote them personal letters, explaining what he saw in their unique personality and skillsets. I received one of those letters. No one had ever told me that I had potential. Twenty years later, he still calls out the greatness in me. When I talked to him on his birthday, he mentioned keeping up with various students. I said, "Al, how many of your old students connect with you regularly?" He paused and said, "A lot." Al tends to minimize his influence, so his response told me everything. I suspect that many of his former students walk a different path because he called out their greatness.

Become familiar with the human needs in this chapter. Apply them even when you are in new and uncertain situations. Imagine that you are facilitating a long meeting. Even if you are unsure of people's feelings about the topic, you know that ensuring a bathroom break will make everyone like you better. Similarly, assuming that everyone has emotional needs creates a positive relational foundation, even when navigating new and uncertain variables. In the next chapter, we will cover tricks to help you read people and indicators to assess the way they think.

KEY TAKEAWAYS

1. *Let people know that they matter, even if you think they already know it.*

2. *If you assume that people want to feel valued, need autonomy, and like to know what to expect, you can optimize most human interactions. Acting on the assumptions will help you reach people who are guarded and unreadable.*

3. *Some people don't recognize their potential. Tell them the strengths you see in them.*

LEADERSHIP APPLICATION

Meeting Needs to Gain Buy-In for Change

If your organization is going through change and you want people to get on board, meet their basic needs. Shouting "Change is good!" and "Transitions are difficult!" is an ineffective shortcut around the real questions people have: "How will this affect me?" "Will I be okay?" "What if I don't get along with the new people?"

Meeting Needs before Team Building

Every year, a cool business book comes out about organizational culture. The ideas are fun but worthless if you don't meet foundational needs. Gold stars alone do not help people to feel valued. Trust falls do not create safety. If you attempt to implement team-building exercises without first meeting basic emotional needs, you are wasting your time. As one of my clients stated about a leader, "We will all go around and answer the question, but we won't get personal. He hasn't earned that."

Chapter 9

HOW TO READ PEOPLE

I n the last chapter, we focused on dominant emotional needs to help you gain a broad understanding of people. This chapter will provide you with information to help you read people in the moment and assess their judgment patterns. The information that people unintentionally disclose through their nonverbals helps us to navigate daily conversations or complex negotiations. The section on assessing other people's judgment is critical for evaluating potential employees, partners, or friends. As you read into the finer points of understanding others, remember to use chapter 8 on fundamental needs as your default if you get confused. When we assume the desires for freedom, acceptance, and safety, we increase our success with people, even if we misread them in the moment.

READING PEOPLE IN THE MOMENT

Reading people in the moment requires attention to their face, tone of voice, body posture, and even attire. If we are distracted by another problem or our internal dialogue, we will miss these cues. Thus, all of the work you've done on understanding your own emotions in chapter 3 and building your personal confidence in chapter 5 will enhance your people-reading skills. You will be less distracted by your emotions, and you'll be focused on the other person instead of your own insecurities. That combination allows us to be fully present and notice the tiny details about others.

Warning: There is a fair amount of literature available to help people make judgments based on nonverbals. I want to caution you on jumping to conclusions. Human interactions are complex, and it is easy to misinterpret situations based on textbook information. For example, someone may glance down when they speak because they are lying. They may also be glancing down because they are shy, thinking, or noticing a bug. At one point in my training, we reviewed videos of client appointments. A male psychologist pointed out a female's hand movement at her torso, along the bra strap. He said, "See her suggestive gesture?" He didn't know that bras can be itchy if they are too tight. Thus, he was misreading an innate response to itching as a sexually suggestive gesture.

In the sections below, I will provide information on several kinds of tells to help you read people, but they are only guidelines. It is dangerous to make assumptions about the meaning of one or two microexpressions. Instead, use them as an indicator to ask questions, to aid communication in high-trust situations, or to assess patterns in high-stakes situations.

Microexpressions

One day, I was role-playing with one of my clients. I deliberately put him on the spot so I could see how he was conveying sensitive information in a professional context.

I interrupted him early in the role-play. "No, no. Your mouth moved." He just stared at me and said, "Okay??? Never mind." I took pity on him and explained.

"Because you are honest, your internal arguments show up on your face and in your voice. Your voice softens; your mouth shifts in a subtle gesture of uncertainty; you lose eye contact. Your face says, 'This is what I'm telling you, but I'm not sure if I believe it myself.' With safe people, it doesn't matter if they read your uncertainty. In this situation, I want you to project only confidence."

Managing our facial expressions is key to protecting ourselves in high-stakes situations with unknown entities (i.e., we are unsure of someone's agenda and trustworthiness). When we can keep our faces neutrally pleasant, we can prevent people from reading us the way I will teach you to read others. Reading the faces of others gives us information that they will never say out loud.

We always hear about the power of nonverbal communication, but we often underutilize it. When we take notes, look at our phone, or otherwise break eye contact, we lose information. You may think that you have problems reading people, but make sure that you are looking at their faces before making that assumption. There are two ways that people betray themselves—through what they reveal and through what they conceal.

Reveal—Tells

I remember giving a client suggestions about how to change her interaction style with a frustrating colleague. I saw her nod in agreement, but I also saw something else.

"What's the 'but'?" I asked.

"What do you mean?" she replied.

"Your eyebrow moved. I don't know what it means. I'm not sure what you were thinking. But something was going on in your mind just now."

The client paused, muttered, "Damn psychologist"...and revealed that she agreed with all of my logic but had an emotional concern.

Negotiators, poker players, and attorneys are familiar with the term "tell." It refers to a subconscious reflexive gesture that reveals a person's emotional state. I have clients who crack their knuckles, adjust their hair, or shift in their seats. Sometimes, I ask about the tell before they realize that they are anxious. People are often unaware of their emotions, and so "tells" can give information outside of even their awareness. Microexpressions are fleeting shifts in facial expressions that are "tells." An eyebrow may twitch, the mouth may move, or pupils may flare.

Changes in breathing patterns are tells. When people get anxious, breaths become shallow. In an audio-only conversation, you might hear a pause in the rhythm or a quick intake of air. The intake of breath is when I pause and ask someone what he or she is thinking. If I ignore that cue, I lose critical information.

The commonality among breathing, eyebrow twitching, and knuckle cracking is that you notice a movement that was not previously there. The change in the pattern rather than the movement itself alerts us to an internal thought process. Even if you think you are horrible at reading others, you can learn to watch for the small changes.

The change in the pattern rather than the movement itself alerts us to an internal thought process.

How to Use Tells in Low-Stakes Situations. In low-stakes, collaborative settings, simply ask people what they are thinking about or if the conversation raised a concern. If they say, "Why do you ask?" note your observation. Refrain from making any assumptions about the reason behind the microexpression or movement. Assumptions can be wrong, insulting, and intrusive. If you are incorrect, people feel misjudged and misunderstood based on body movement. They may also feel that you are invading their privacy. When you simply ask, people feel safe. They know that you are observant, but the very act of asking lets them know that you will not jump to conclusions.

Script:
You: "Wait, did I say something confusing?"
Him: "No, I don't think so."
You: "Oh, okay, I saw something in your face and thought
      that maybe I wasn't explaining it clearly."
or
You: "Are you okay?"
Her: "Yeah, why?"

You: "Something seemed a little off, but honestly, it could
   have been a trick of the light."

or

You: "Wait, did I say something to upset you?"

Him: "No."

You: "Okay, I just thought I saw something on your face, but
   I was probably wrong."

What do all of the scripts have in common? You mention the
microexpression and take the pressure off of the other person to
respond. The speech is casual, and you provide a possible explanation that doesn't put others on the spot. Usually, people will think
for a second and then explain that you did say something that
caused the reaction or that they were responding to a nonrelated
stimulus (back pain, hunger, a moment of distraction).

Sometimes I don't want to call out the tells because I don't want
to derail the conversation. If I am trying to help someone problem-solve in a time-limited situation, I want to ignore the tell so
that we can stay on track and achieve the goal. Whenever I pause to
ask about the tell, I uncover information that was drastically more
important than the dialogue at hand.

If you are productivity- and time-focused like me, add margin
into your agendas to inquire about the tells. Otherwise, you may
cover all of the information you thought was important and none
of the information that could actually change the game.

In group settings, you may not want to call something out in
the middle of a meeting. If you note a fleeting microexpression, ask
afterward.

Script: "Hey, I saw something on your face when I was talking about X, but I don't know if it was about my topic or something else. I just wanted to check in if I said something offensive or confusing."

How to Use Tells in High-Stakes Situations. In high-stakes situations, pretend that you are not watching. If you are funny, sarcastic, or effervescently happy, use the colorful personality characteristic to your advantage. Many people will automatically attend to these variables and miss or underestimate the degree to which you are simultaneously paying attention to their reactions. If people know that you are watching, they will automatically manage their tells, so do your best to mask your observations.

On the other hand, if the goal is to be intimidating, watch people and let them see you watching them. This strategy signifies authority, confidence, and inside knowledge. If they respond to your power play by becoming nervous, closing up, or otherwise self-protecting, they give you additional tells about their level of confidence in the interaction. If they do not appear intimidated, they may have nothing to hide. Alternately, they have information that gives them the upper hand.

Conceal—the Absence of Expression

Remember that I said it is the change in pattern, rather than the tell itself? Another "tell" is the absolute absence of expression. You won't see any changes, because the face remains neutral. A lengthy neutral countenance indicates an attempt to conceal. The people who know me well understand that my facial neutrality signals a problem. Why? I am intense and expressive. I may modulate both attributes according to the situation, but I only adopt a neutral expression or a polite smile when I am wholly and intentionally masking my thoughts.

It is easier to identify concealment when we already know people's patterns, but how do you do so with acquaintances or strangers? Pay attention to their eyes and other parts of their bodies. They will usually reveal something despite their efforts to conceal. If they are completely blank, it means that they have disengaged from you or that something is wrong. If their facial expression remains the same for an extended period, they may be distracted or masking, even if they are smiling. We naturally have a little bit of a reaction to information that is interesting or emotionally stimulating. Some people are less expressive, but a flat affect over a 30-minute conversation means something. You won't know what it means. You can either ask the person if he or she has a different perspective or simply hold the observation for your future reference.

Attire Cues

One of my friends often wears unique ties. If I met him for the first time, I would know that he has a sense of whimsy or is attached to someone who gives him fun ties. Both explanations get me to the emotional side of him separate from the message in the rest of the business suit. The degree to which a person's attire gives you cues varies according to the situation. Some people work in settings that dictate conservative and traditional styles, even though this is not their personality. Someone may wear a flowered shirt simply because it's the only clean one in his closet. Attire does not give you answers; it's another place to raise questions. The inconsistencies are the areas that give me the most information. Specifically, if I see someone in nondescript suits or casual wear, with some cool socks, jewelry, or ties, the contrast gives information. I understand that they conform to traditional expectations but may have a unique personality. Then I can figure out if what I'm noting is related to extra warmth, a value for uniqueness, individuality, or a sense of whimsy.

READING PEOPLE'S JUDGMENT PATTERNS

Reading people in the moment optimizes interactions. We can learn about their overall behavior by reading judgment patterns. We discussed learning whom to trust in chapter 7 to assess whether people are emotionally safe. When we learn their judgment patterns, we can assess whether they are the right fit for extended personal or professional relationships.

For 14 years, I had a loving, sweet cat named Princess. She was my baby. (Even if you hate cats, stick with me on the story; there's a lesson here.) One night I went on a date, and the subject of cats came up. I told my date about Princess, and he told me that his father gave him a dollar per head to shoot kittens when he was six years old. My date went on to say that it started getting hard by the fifth or sixth kitten. We didn't have a second date. Why? It wasn't just that he shot kittens. Even though the story was upsetting, I understood that he was a child. What did concern me was his judgment. Why would he tell a woman with a cat named Princess that he had shot baby kittens?

Some of the best advice I received about supervising others was from the director of my PhD program. "You know, Tricia," she said, "I don't worry much about one mistake because everyone makes mistakes. I worry if a mistake or pattern of mistakes reflects a judgment problem. You can teach skills, but you can't teach judgment."

Judgment patterns help you discern if someone can effectively manage your business, organization, confidential information, or a high-stakes situation. Below are some of the common areas where problems in judgment may affect the outcomes of your personal or business relationships.

Executive-Functioning Judgment Problems

Did you ever work with someone who seemed blind to the consequences of decisions or acted impulsively without thinking through potential outcomes? Executive functioning occurs in the very front part of the brain, called our prefrontal cortex. It helps us problem-solve, strategize, and plan elaborate sequences of antecedent-consequence ("if-then") scenarios. People with poor executive functioning are often viewed as stupid or lacking common sense. Either they don't do something critical to success, or they take an action that guarantees failure. The fallacies in their decision-making process are apparent to the objective observer.

The prefrontal cortex also contains the "braking" mechanisms that help us with impulse control. When we have impulse control, we can pause before reacting. We may be angry, but we recognize the need to keep our anger in check. We may want something immediately, but we decide our action based on the longer-term ramifications.

Assess executive reasoning when you are making choices about the people you want to involve in leadership, high-stakes situations, or personal endeavors. It is critical to your sanity and your outcome. Because errors in "judgment" happen at a neurological level, it usually takes a trained professional to assist with executive dysfunction. Recognizing any problems with executive judgment helps us assign people to the right tasks such that we do not set them up for failure or misinterpret the deficit as a character flaw.

Indicators of Executive Dysfunction

1. Complex tasks, those requiring the integration of many details, will overwhelm the person, creating a freeze response. You will notice what appears to be procrastination.

2. You coach the person to use a different method or to "think ahead," but you can't seem to make him or her understand.

3. In decision-making, the person attends only to the variables that are immediately at hand. He or she does not account for the factors that may arise four steps out.

4. This person is unable to assess multiple facets of the same problem.

Two areas of daily functioning that may be affected by executive dysfunction include risk judgment and planning judgment.

Risk Judgment.

Signs.

1. Someone takes actions that will inevitably create problems but is blind to the adverse outcomes. The person does not see the downsides of a decision until you explain them.

2. If you ask the person to assess the potential consequences of actions, he or she may focus on a minor negative outcome and miss a critical factor.

Assessment Questions for Risk Judgment.

1. Do the person's actions create chaos?

2. Is this person able to assess risk and then devise a plan to mitigate it?

3. Could you trust this person to thoroughly examine the factors of an important decision and create an appropriate plan of action? (It doesn't need to be the way you would do it, but it needs to appear logical and derived from all of the variables at hand.)

Planning Judgment.

Signs.

1. People with executive dysfunction flounder with prioritizing tasks and time management. Everyone grapples with these items, but a deficit in executive functioning impairs daily functioning and rudimentary task completion.

2. You'll often notice difficulty and confusion surrounding the person's ability to keep appointments and remember meetings.

Assessment Questions for Planning Judgment.

1. Is this person able to figure out the best use of time?

2. Does this person allocate time according to the priorities, or does he or she allow "mood" to dictate time usage?

3. Can this person plan and execute tasks, appointments, and meetings?

4. Can this person think ahead to future tasks and backtrack the sequence into a daily plan?

Social Judgment. Social judgment combines emotional intelligence and healthy personal functioning. A person with excellent social judgment knows how to interact effectively and has the personal capacity to implement that knowledge. Social judgment is critical to navigating sensitive or political situations, such that you want to account for this variable if you are placing leaders in high-visibility or high-stakes contexts. Your organization will be extra vulnerable to litigation if you have a leader with poor discernment. "I didn't mean anything by it" doesn't seem to dispel lawsuits. On the personal side, your life will simply be happier if you surround yourself with people who have appropriate social judgment. No matter how well intentioned, people with poor social judgment tend to add stress to relationships.

Assessment Questions for Social Judgment.

1. Can I trust this person to hold information confidential? (If the person shares other people's secrets, the answer is no. You are not unique.)

2. Can I trust this person to know what information is appropriate to share or not share in various contexts? (If you cringe because the person makes inappropriate jokes in the wrong setting, the answer is no.)

3. Can I trust this person to think before he or she speaks, or is there a tendency to say whatever comes to mind?

4. Will this person be able to navigate other personality styles with diplomacy?

5. Does this person have appropriate boundaries?

6. Is this person aware of how others perceive his or her behavior?

Emotional Judgment. A person's ability to control his or her emotions will affect the surrounding people. When you choose work and personal relationships, think about the degree to which people can positively manage their emotions.

Assessment Questions for Emotional Judgment.

1. Is this person able to manage his or her emotions such that you can reasonably predict mood?

2. Is this person able to modulate emotion according to the context, people, and stakes involved?

3. Does this person own his or her emotions, or does he or she displace them onto everyone else?

4. Is this person able to separate emotions from decision-making? Everyone gets emotional, but it is good to recognize when our emotions are so high that they may cloud our decision-making. Someone with good judgment will realize the vulnerability and allow emotions to cool first.

Financial Judgment. Problems with financial judgment have ended personal and professional relationships. Financial decisions arise from a complex intersection of personal history, financial values, emotions, risk-tolerance, executive functioning, and social pressures. It is far better to assess a person's financial judgment before deciding to engage in a relationship than try to resolve incompatibility later. Personal finances will impact business. Business partners may "borrow" from the company to cover personal misspending. Employees may push for an unwarranted raise to offset personal financial concerns. Owners may make risky business decisions due to desperation in their personal finances.

Assessment Questions for Financial Judgment.
1. Is this person able to prioritize spending according to longer-term goals?

2. Does this person's behavior correspond with the prioritizations?

3. Does this person spend money on unnecessary items for the business?

4. Is this person able to make decisions based on numbers instead of emotion?

Reading people in the moment allows us to communicate more effectively and hold information for future reference. Assessing judgment helps us know what we can expect from their future actions and make decisions accordingly. In the next chapter, you will learn how to read personality-specific needs and respond to others' behavior.

KEY TAKEAWAYS

1. *Reading people requires focus. If you are distracted, you will miss the cues they present.*

2. *Assess cognitive, social, emotional, and financial judgment processes before engaging in substantive personal or professional relationships.*

LEADERSHIP APPLICATION

Reading People One on One

Focus on their face. Maintain eye contact. You can read microexpressions in person and on video. If you are taking notes on paper or at a computer, you will likely miss some expressions. If time is tight, you may see the microexpression but be too focused on the schedule to pause and ask about it. Whenever possible, inquire about the microexpression. The information you'll obtain may supersede or inform the rest of your agenda.

Reading the Room

Watch people's reactions to other people's statements. Notice how far apart people are sitting and how their bodies are angled. Apart from what they say, notice when they speak, when they don't speak, and changes in tone or expression. Watch the people with whom they make eye contact.

Internal Barriers to Reading People

We have to be present to read people. If we are distracted by other issues or by our concerns about what they are thinking of us, or if we are focused on problem-solving the content at hand, we will miss microexpressions. It's normal for these interruptions to occur, but reading people means splitting awareness between your agenda and theirs.

Discerning Mistakes versus Judgment Problems

We can remediate mistake making; we cannot fix judgment. Mistakes result from a lack of knowledge or inattention to detail. When team members make mistakes, ask them to walk you through the rationale for their decisions or actions. Do not ask leading questions; just listen. The answers will let you know if it was a mistake or if it reflects poor judgment.

Judgment Problems Create Litigation Risk

You create risk for yourself and your organization when you allow people with judgment problems to remain in your sphere. If you have a business partner with a judgment problem, seek legal counsel on steps you can take to protect yourself. I'm going to hurt your feelings here for a minute—if you know that poor judgment is a factor and you decide to overlook it, you have a judgment problem.

Chapter 10

HOW TO READ MOTIVATION AND CHANGE BEHAVIOR

L et me disappoint you first. I can't tell you how to change people. Remember, people are who they are, not who you want them to be. Even though you can successfully change many things in your life or business, you can't change people's core traits. You can get better at reading the primary motivations, applying behavioral principles, and learning the unconscious principles that guide interactions.

You'll notice that some of the examples in this chapter assume professional settings. High achievers believe that a failure to change their colleagues or subordinates is a failure in leadership. Yes, you can influence people, and I will share tactics on how to optimize interpersonal outcomes. At the same time, remember that people's actions are mostly outside of your control.

READING MOTIVATIONS

"How do I understand what motivates people, Tricia?" my client asked. The question comes up a lot, usually from high achievers who are flummoxed by the apparent apathy of their subordinates. I always tell them that I don't know how to motivate a truly unmotivated person. What I do know, and what I can share here, is how to bring out the best in people by knowing what they value.

Incorporating the knowledge of what people find rewarding will increase their existing motivation. Below is a list of values and how to recognize them in people. Note that we all value these to some extent, but we place them at different importance levels.

1. **Status.** This person works hard for recognition. He may speak about accomplishments or name-drop others in the power hierarchy. He may seek to express success through his attire, car, or other outward accouterments. (Values titles, promotions, public validation.)

2. **Approval.** This person wants to be liked and fears being judged. He always agrees with you or the group. If the room is in disagreement, this person will be silent because he does not want to alienate anyone. This person frequently apologizes, even if he has no responsibility for the mistake. (Values compliments, awards, and ongoing reassurance.)

3. **Desire to Perform Correctly (Linked to Approval).** This person needs to know the precise expectations and

requirements for a task. She will ask for the structure,
timeline, and details. The emotional need is to do the
job correctly to be approved of as a person or live up to
personal standards. The link is not bidirectional; some
people need approval or personal excellence but are
not detail-oriented and precise. (Values clear, specific,
sequential instructions. Lack of feedback makes her
anxious.)

4. **Autonomy/Freedom.** This person is often the first to
offer a different opinion in a group situation. She is not
likely to ask for permission or validation from others
before acting. If this person is positive and collaborative,
she can be a proactive asset. If she simply likes doing
things independently without regard to the group, do
not hire her if you need a team player. (Values control
over the way she does her job; values freedom in
decision-making.)

5. **Challenge.** This person thrives on new projects and loves
to win. He will volunteer for new initiatives and will
embrace competition. If he does not have the opportunity
to grow, he will move on to a more stimulating
environment. (Values new opportunities, innovation,
self-mastery.)

6. **Peace.** This person always finds a way to interrupt or
dampen conflict and help two sides see each other's

perspective. In high-conflict situations, this person may emotionally shut down, such that she stops engaging. (Values a harmonious work environment with an easygoing boss and colleagues.)

Application of Motivations and Needs

When you note that someone seems to be high in a specific category, orient conversations and reinforcements to that motivation. For example, someone who needs explicit details of tasks to obtain value through performing becomes highly anxious with a laissez-faire supervisor. A person who wants approval will be motivated toward better performance with positive reinforcement. Someone who has a high need for status may value a higher title more than a financial incentive.

LEADERSHIP APPLICATION

Enhancing Workplace Motivation

The above motivations link to differences in personality styles. Regardless of these differences, people work best when they have the resources to do the job and the opportunity to excel. When motivated people feel like their hands are tied, they naturally decrease their effort to ameliorate the pain of working hard without results. People become similarly frustrated if they feel left out of essential communication. Ask people regularly if they have everything they need to do their jobs.

Provide them with growth opportunities. Some people will welcome new areas of responsibility and promotions; others might prefer individual curricula. My dental hygienist loves the book club at her company; she feels like they are investing in her growth. Ownership also increases motivation. Whether people lead the safety committee or create new office solutions, they can see the tangible value they bring to the organization.

HOW TO CHANGE BEHAVIOR

I want to bang my head against the wall when someone says, "I guess I'll have to talk to him again." The comment is always about a subordinate. The leader has already "talked to" the subordinate two times before. "Talking to" someone for the third time will not make a difference. Okay, I got that off my chest. If this is you, I still think you're fabulous; I just want you to change your approach.

We rely on language to maintain our relationships, so we expect language to change other people's behavior. Sometimes clear communication does result in change, especially if you are talking to a coachable person. However, if you have already said the same thing three times, a fourth conversation will not change the game. So what do we do when words don't work? You will need to add behavioral strategies.

Training Dogs, Cats, and People

I used to be diplomatic when I talked about changing people's behavior. When I was a therapist, my clients wanted to change the behavior of their spouses, friends, and children. As an executive coach, they want to change the behavior of their colleagues, investors, partners, or employees (and their spouses, friends, and children). I tried to be sensitive as I laid out the fundamentals of behavior change. At some point, my clients read the fine print between my sentences and said,

"You're telling me I should treat ___ like a dog."

Now, when people say, "How do I change him or her?" I respond, "Do you have a cat or a dog? If so, we train people the same way."

Even if you have never owned a pet, think about this. How many things would you do consistently with no internal or external reward? Would you go to the gym if you gained weight? Would you continue to work if you didn't get paid? Would you volunteer for your charity if no one seemed to appreciate it? Reinforcement (reward) increases behavior—whether it is in cats, dogs, or humans. Even when we act according to internal motivation or moral standards, our actions make us feel good about ourselves, thereby providing positive reinforcement.

All of us need to have a combination of reinforcement and punishment at our disposal. In the same way that one discovers what is uniquely effective to train children, cats, and dogs, we have to figure out how to train the people in our environment. Implementing behavioral strategies reinforces those who are internally wired toward excellence and provides boundaries for those who are not. Below are examples of reinforcers and punishments in the work setting. Behavioral strategies work best if we understand what people value, so we can train them more effectively.

Examples of reinforcements in a work setting (rewards that increase a positive behavior) include the following:

1. Compliments (still words, but they speak to the human need to be valued)

2. Increased influence (leading a project with appropriate status or financial recognition)

3. Increased autonomy (controlling work hours or environment)

4. Increased latitude (the ability to create something new or try an idea)

5. Group approval

6. Chocolate

7. Bonuses

Reinforcing positive actions is often an efficient path to behavioral change. In our discussion on human needs, I emphasized the need for people to feel valued and accepted. Catching others doing something right and reinforcing them will often increase good behavior across motivational categories. I explained this strategy to one of my clients. When I gave him chocolate at the end of the appointment, he said, "Wait, you're doing it to us, aren't you? You're giving us chocolate to reinforce us!" Guilty.

What do you do if positive reinforcement doesn't work? If the bad behavior itself is rewarding, a person will continue the behavior unless consequences make it less attractive.

Examples of punishment in the workplace include the following *(Note: Punishment decreases behavior because we add something negative or remove something positive.)*:

1. Written warning (negative added: fear)

2. Day off without pay (removal of positive: money)

3. A succinct reprimand such as "Please put down your phone when Maria is presenting" (negative added: public reprimand). *When we allow repeated bad behavior in group settings, we risk the morale and cohesion of the group.*

4. Verbal disappointment (removal of positive: approval). *This only works if someone values your approval.*

5. Restriction of autonomy and choice, decreasing scope of responsibility or restricting work flexibility (removal of positive: autonomy and choice)

6. Lack of response to requests for reassurance (removal of positive: peace of mind)

Delineate the relationship between the person's poor performance and punishment. Don't expect them to "get it."

Script: "You have continued to take advantage of flexible work hours such that you are not meeting your obligations. At this point, you need to ask me permission for all changes to your schedule."

"What Do I Do When Nothing Works?"

As a leader, you need to make the call about how much energy you will spend on someone who is underperforming or misbehaving. Someone who does not respond to direct feedback and reinforcements or disciplinary actions is not a good fit for your environment. All of the energy you spend diminishes your ability to invest in the people or processes that will drive the company forward. Sometimes one of my clients focuses on saving an unsalvageable employee, and we spend hours on that employee instead of critical initiatives. This approach is another example of letting someone "win twice." You have to deal with their underperformance, and then you pay them by giving them your sleep, your waking focus, your time, and the morale of your other employees. If you argue that this person is indispensable, what would you do if he or she quit or became ill? Use that strategy to backtrack into a solution.

Many organizations have performance improvement or corrective action plans that occur before terminating an individual. This strategy can be helpful for coachable employees or those with specific skill deficits. Performance improvement plans will not resolve personality problems. In many cases, a 360 evaluation that includes feedback on soft skills can pave the way for terminating someone who is simply a bad fit. My best advice is always to consult with HR early when the red flags first appear. Make sure that you have a clear understanding of the specific actions and timelines associated with termination so that you can plan accordingly. (Go to *www.relational genius.com* for additional resources.)

RESPONDING TO OTHERS' BAD BEHAVIOR IN THE MOMENT

I work with a lot of analytical high achievers who comment, "I never know what to say in the moment when someone is rude. I freeze. Afterward, I think of 100 things I could have said." It is hard to find the right words in the middle of emotionally charged situations.

Think about it. For all of us, the process requires:

1. noting the other person's comment or behavior;

2. identifying what we feel;

3. figuring out the words to describe it;

4. then stating a need/desire/position,

5. in a language that the other person understands,

6. while simultaneously accounting for all of the variables in the situation,

7. in order to rapidly assess and discard possible verbal responses,

8. in order to choose the right one that will result in the optimal long-term outcome.

Phew. I'm tired already. The process of translating emotions into words involves multiple parts of both our left and right brains—communicating between each other in milliseconds (to name a few—Broca's, Wernicke's, angular gyrus, insular cortex, amygdala, hypothalamus). The complexities associated with speaking optimally in high-emotion and high-consequence scenarios call for two specific tools: (a) one-liners at our disposal and (b) a method of creating a pause.

One-Liners

One-liners are short sentences that you can use in a variety of situations. If you memorize just a few of them, your brain can access them even when you are upset. In Part IV, you will learn a plethora of one-liners to use for Difficult People. In Part V, you'll find one-liner options for a wider variety of situations. If you don't see one that fits, brainstorm ideas with a friend. When you find one-liners that work, practice saying them until you can use them fluently. Ask someone you trust to role-play being a jerk so that you can practice saying the one-liners, even when someone renders you speechless.

Some of my favorites:

"Everyone has an opinion."
"You could be right."
"That's my decision."

A one-liner that disengages you from the conversation cuts off the oxygen of someone who is acting up. As a leader, you will find them especially useful if you have a subordinate who persistently argues your decisions.

The Magic Trick

If you are in a situation where someone will not take no for an answer, continues to push an argument, or otherwise does not seem to "hear" you, repeat the same sentence in the same sequence, three times. If you have a one-liner at your disposal, keep repeating it. Do not change your tone inflection or your expression. Do not add words or try to explain. If you deviate verbally or non-verbally, the other person will perceive the deviation as a crack in your stance.

I have noted this trick in part V on scripts because it works with everything from a hassling salesperson to a high-stakes negotiation. It also works with Difficult People, as noted in Part IV. At the risk of being redundant, I am including it here to ensure that you see it.

When we say the same thing, in the same sequence, we catch the other person's attention. We all naturally change speech rhythms or word sequence when we explain something the second time. When we don't, we send a signal of implacability to the other person. One of my clients used this tactic and reported back, "Tricia, I couldn't believe it! It was like magic. They didn't know what to do!" When I role-play this strategy with my clients, I usually get them to crack by the third time, such that they change their words, face, or tone. If you can master the art of total consistency through three repetitions, you will feel powerful, and the other person will feel like he is running into a brick wall.

Creating a Pause

Creating a pause helps us respond to the general population. It is critical when you deal with Difficult People. Hence, I want to introduce it here, and then follow up on its protective power in Part IV.

I've noticed that most of us feel like we need to have an immediate response to an accusation. Some people are very good at pushing our emotional buttons, such that we feel the need to respond. A reactive response can play right into their hands and add oxygen to the blaze. Even when no one has malicious intentions, creating a pause protects us from overpromising, setting an unwanted precedent, or "showing our cards."

Pausing becomes critical in emotionally charged or high-stakes situations. If a challenging conversation occurred, you might need time to allow the emotion to de-escalate. Arbitrarily, I suggest waiting 24 hours to a few days before returning to the discussion. If you wait longer than a week, it will be difficult for the other person to remember the points, context, and emotions. This rule of thumb is especially important if you are upset and the other person has no awareness of the fact. Further, after a week, they may not recall the conversation. You will both be frustrated and have difficulty finding a resolution if they can't remember the dialogue.

The pause is intentional, and it ends. It is not an excuse to procrastinate. If you find yourself procrastinating on returning to the topic, it means that you don't want to have the conversation, even though you should. As we noted previously, interpersonal challenges don't go away. Left unattended, they create infections. If you miss the window, you don't have to deal with potential conflict, but you also miss the opportunity to prevent the sepsis.

When I find myself dreading a necessary conversation, I cope with the emotional resistance by telling myself the truth. "Tricia, there will never be a time that feels good. You will never actually want to have this conversation." Then I grumble, complain, take a deep breath, and do everything I'm telling you to do.

MAINTAINING PERSPECTIVE ABOUT OTHERS' BEHAVIOR

It's normal to assume that both the type and intensity of others' behavior occurs as a response to us. This assumption constrains problem-solving because we do not assess other contributing variables. Further, we add stress when we assume responsibility for outcomes outside of our control. Maintaining awareness of outside factors and potential hot-button reactions helps us develop a more nuanced response to others' behavior.

It's Not about You

These quotes reflect our automatic assumptions that someone else's behavior is our fault.

"She pushed back when I gave her instructions. She obviously doesn't respect me."

"They question my recommendations. I must be doing a bad job explaining, or they don't respect my expertise."

"I warned her that this would break up her marriage. She didn't believe me. Could I have said anything differently?"

The last example is mine. For years, I got frustrated when I wanted to protect clients from the consequences of their own decisions and they ignored my warnings. I had given them reasons, research, and experience. When they ignored my warnings, I second-guessed myself—did I not explain correctly? I was frustrated with them, but deep inside, I thought it was about me.

Finally, I asked for feedback from the person whose marital failure I had predicted two years in advance. I had initially said, "I know that things are great now, but I've seen this pattern before. I highly recommend that you do ____, or your marriage will be on the rocks two years from now." She didn't take the suggestion; they got divorced. I decided to ask the question:

> *Tricia:* "Could I have done or said anything different to you?"

> *Client:* "No. I remember the conversation. I remember what you said. And what I thought was, *Oh, she is talking about someone else. She's not talking about me.*"

It is natural for us to believe that others' reactions to us are about us. Our brains automatically assess the variables in the situation and understandably overestimate our impact. Yet in doing so, we draw inaccurate conclusions. We never know the backstories of the people around us. They come with their own beliefs, their own expectations, and their own needs. We are only involved in a sliver of the story, and it is usually the whole story, rather than the slice, that drives their interactions with us.

Suppose you ask someone you like a simple question, and he gets defensive. You may assume that you approached it the wrong way or that the friendship isn't as close as you thought. Here are some possible reasons for his defensive tone that have nothing to do with you.

1. He doesn't have an answer to the question, and he thinks he should.

2. Someone else criticized him on a related topic.

3. He was thinking about a fight with his wife during your conversation.

4. He hasn't eaten for 8 hours, and he is edgy.

5. Your question caught him off guard. He is confused, not defensive.

Hot Buttons

Occasionally, a rational person has an over-the-top response to a situation. We may notice we occasionally do the same. With a frustrating circumstance, a typical emotional reaction might be an 8 or 9 on a 1 to 10 scale of intensity. When someone responds at a level 15, you can assume the presence of a hot button. Hot buttons, called "triggers" in psych jargon, develop from previous traumas. Logically, we may understand that the current situation is different from the traumatic experience; emotionally, it feels the same. The "trauma" is not necessarily death, accident, or assault. It might be a history of being bullied, minimized, criticized, or other experiences that created distress about our core self. A response from someone that seems disproportionate to the situation indicates that we have inadvertently triggered thoughts and emotions linked to those earlier experiences. (If someone routinely reacts with extreme amounts of negative emotion, you are not merely dealing with hot buttons. There are deeper psychological issues present.)

What to Do in Hot-Button Situations

If you sense that you may have hit a hot button in someone else, simply apologize for the upset, then come back a few days later.

Immediate Script: "I am sorry. I think I said something that hurt you, and that was not my intention."

Hot-button reactions take time to diminish. Show the person you care. Then provide space. Check in after a day or so to debrief the interaction.

Later Script: "I wanted to check in with you about our conversation on Tuesday. I think I miscommunicated something. It was not my intention to offend you."

Notice that the above script focuses on your possible miscommunication. Pull the focus back on yourself rather than digging for an answer or trying to understand the other person's reaction. Hot buttons make people extremely vulnerable. They may not want to explain the reaction, especially in work settings. Take whatever response they give you, and simply let them know that you care.

If someone hits your hot button, give yourself time to recover, and figure out what got triggered. One of my clients, who prided himself in his emotional containment, was appalled when someone hit his hot button. I had to break the news that he is human and that most of us have them. There are therapeutic strategies to decrease the intense reactions to hot buttons. This solution is beneficial if you have many hot buttons or if the responses get in the way of your daily functioning. Otherwise, if the hot button is occasional and incurs minimal damage, just understand what the button is and why it is there, and give yourself time to process through the emotion of it.

PROJECTION, NEGATIVE FEEDBACK LOOPS, AND SCRIPTS

Hot buttons, unrecognized, can create conflict and extended sequences of negative interactions. Projection, negative feedback loops, and scripts can also erode relationships. If you understand these phenomena, you have the power to prevent conflict and alter entrenched negative interactions.

I learned about the phenomenon of projection in my Psychology 100 class. For several years, I dismissed it as another weird hypothesis from Sigmund Freud. Textbooks will tell you that projection is a defense mechanism, and then when you look up that term, you have to read about Freud's sexual obsession...it's just a mess.

So, let me give you the definition without all the extra nonsense. Projection is this: when we dislike people, we assume they dislike us. If we are disappointed in people, we start thinking that they are disappointed in us. If we are angry at someone, we say, "I'm sure they hate us." This thought process can start a negative feedback loop. When we make these assumptions, our emotions cause subtle shifts in our behavior. Their brains notice this shift, and they begin responding differently as well. The negative feedback loop continues, and the relationship deteriorates, even if we never argue.

The negative feedback loop becomes the footwork to a well-rehearsed dance called a script. We begin to follow a script without thinking about it. Think of someone you know well—your partner, a work colleague, or a close friend with whom you have a recurring argument. I bet that if I asked you, you could tell me how the fight begins, builds, and ends. I have asked people to switch roles in well-known arguments, and they can repeat line for line what the other person will say. When I ask people to do this, they start laughing because they see the absurdity of it. They are following a script. The script says, "Annie says _____. Then I say _____. Then she says this. I say _____."

Scripts can be verbal or behavioral sequences. If I invite you into my office and say, "Make yourself comfortable," you will sit in a chair. You will not sit on the floor. You will not stand. You will not sit in my lap. Society taught you a long time ago that the behavior you should follow is to sit in a chair.

We act on scripts every day without conscious awareness. From a neurological standpoint, scripts reduce our cognitive load. Our brains automatically find rules and efficiencies to maximize our attentional resources. If I don't have to think about every word and every action, I can focus on other items. **Since everyone follows scripts without conscious awareness, we can alter scripts and change the situation without ever having a conversation.**

Changing the Scripts—Bring Them Brownies

One of my clients was in a volatile legal situation. The client was hard-edged, stubborn, and sometimes arrogant. He was well intentioned on the inside, but he hid it well. We debriefed multiple tension-filled meetings. I wanted to tell him to bring everyone brownies, but I held back, honestly afraid that he would think I was utterly insane. (This was earlier in my career when I still wanted my clients to think I was normal.)

One day, he walked into my office, and I inquired about the latest vitriolic encounter.

"You know what, Tricia? I did something different this time. I bought some chocolate, and I brought it to the meeting."

I smiled on the inside. "And what happened?" I asked.

"It changed the entire meeting," he said. "Everyone immediately relaxed. We covered the same topics, but the tone was noticeably friendlier. It seemed like we were communicating as people instead of as adversaries."

The adversarial dance is an extremely well-scripted one. I am good; you are bad. You are the enemy. I need to defend myself or crush you. I hate you; you hate me. We will trade accusations or sit in stony silence. There is nothing in that script that suggests bringing chocolate, giving a compliment, or offering to help. When I interject an unexpected element, I disrupt the feedback loop and change the script.

Years ago, one of my colleagues used this method when she argued with her spouse. She said that she walked up and kissed him in the middle of the argument. I loved it. "What happened?" I asked. She responded, "He got flustered, didn't know what to do, and the argument died out."

Applying Script Change

Scenario 1—Rational People. The other players are well intentioned; you are simply in conflict.

- **Options:** Reach to the other person's humanity. Bring brownies. Offer to help. Kiss your partner in the middle of an argument. Acknowledge the other person's point of view.

- **Benefits:** The other person will relax. The tension decreases. The ensuing conversation is likely to be more productive.

- **Warnings:** *Do not* do this with someone who is entitled or a bully (discussed in Part IV). They will misinterpret it as agreement, think that you are a pushover, or believe that they have won. If you sense that a person is toxic or evil, see the appropriate script below.

- **Argument and Counterargument:**
  Client: "But, Tricia, I don't want to be fake. That
  feels uncomfortable. They might think that I am
  manipulative."
  Tricia:
    - "What you are doing isn't working, is it?"
    - "Do you want to be comfortable, or do you want to
      change the situation?"
    - "Okay, so prevent them from thinking that you are
      manipulative. Call out the conflict. 'I know that we
      are at odds on this, but I still think you're a great
      person. I brought us brownies.'"

Scenario 2—Toxic or Evil People. The other players are snakes.
You don't trust them. They are power-hungry.

- **Options:** The options below are similar to those that
  bullies use—confuse, intimidate, and keep people off-
  balance. You can modify them to your liking, as long as you
  do not soften your presentation.
    - Get a glass pigeon; put it on his or her desk. When
      asked why you put it there, say, "It seemed like the right
      thing to do." (My friend was confused when she read
      this because she thought that "glass pigeon" was a term.
      Maybe I'll coin it. Glass pigeon: an object or action
      that is purposefully used out of context, thus creating

confusion or curiosity.)

- Ask one of them if he had a hamster when he was growing up. When he asks why you are asking, shrug nonchalantly and say, "I just wondered."
- Be as unpredictable as possible. Ego-stroke one week; avoid contact the next.

- **Benefits:** You gain power because the other person assumes that you have intentions. They think that you are playing a game and become insecure. In their insecurity, they will either distance themselves or show their cards.

- **Warnings:**
  1. *Do not* explain anything. Stay confident. Don't react. Hold your cards close. Remain implacable.
  2. They will often begin treating you better. If you are a nice person, you will want to respond in kind. You will trust too quickly and show your cards. In doing this, you will lose power and reduce your ability to manage them in the future.

- **Argument and Counterargument:**
  Client: "But, Tricia, they will think I'm crazy."
  Tricia: "Perfect. People are scared of crazy."
  Client: "But, Tricia, I want to be up-front and treat people the way I want them to treat me."
  Tricia: "Am I asking you to harm them? No. A strange object, a shrug, or a weird question is not hurtful.

Further, you can't play their game with your default rules." (See Part IV on dealing with Difficult People.)

The Power of Scripts in Forming Expectations

One of my clients had an ongoing issue with two employees. He and I discussed the situation multiple times. After the employees made two serious mistakes, my client told them, in a group setting, that he would fire them if the same behavior occurred again. I asked if he would follow through, noting that he would lose the whole group's respect if he did not. He responded that he doesn't make threats unless he is prepared to act. In addition to the threat of termination, he also sent a warning letter with clearly delineated objectives that the employees needed to meet. A week later, he asked his administrative assistant to coordinate the two employees to present at his office for a 30-minute meeting on a Friday afternoon. What happened next? If you've been in a corporate environment, you know that the employees got fired, because that's what happens on Friday afternoons.

The employees walked out of the meeting, and a bystander noted that they both appeared shell-shocked. What actually happened in that meeting? My client told them that they had met the weekly objectives and wanted to follow up as he had promised. He told them to go home early and enjoy their families.

I laughed. I still laugh every time I think about it. My client did not understand why I was laughing. You see, he did not have a mental script that firing occurs on Fridays. He was simply following up on a promise, and Friday was when he had the time to do so. I believe he gained a lot of influential power that day—that he is fair, consistent, and may not follow the scripts that other people expect.

The Power Loss of Being a Predictable Script

It's easy for us to play one note. If we are "pushovers," people will not take us seriously. If we make threats without action, people will not take us seriously. However, suppose we can be reliable overall but tailor our responses to each situation? In that case, people intuitively understand that there is a boundary that they cannot cross. When I told my client in the above scenario that the surprise Friday meeting had given him power, he hesitated. He has worked hard to be a fair, steady, and consistent leader. "Is that a good thing?" he asked.

Generally, we do want people to know what to expect. If we surprise people at random, we come across as loose cannons. When people don't know what to expect, it violates the need for safety discussed earlier. At the same time, complete predictability makes people take us for granted. The unintentional power move that my client made, by trying to be a good leader, was that he showed a willingness to change his approach when the change is warranted. He gives grace and second chances when they are justified; he is equally willing to call an end to the game if people aren't playing well.

KEY TAKEAWAYS

1. It's not about you. When we assume that someone else's behavior is not directly linked to their thoughts about us, we are less likely to be hurt, defensive, or angry. Communication stays open, and we are in a better position to respond appropriately if we do find out that it's about us.

2. *Talking to someone is not a consequence.*

3. *People act according to well-rehearsed scripts without conscious awareness. Doing something unusual to interfere with that script provides space for change.*

LEADERSHIP APPLICATION

Preventing Negative Feedback Loops When Giving Feedback

When you provide negative or "constructive" feedback, stay focused on the specifics. *Do not* make the mistake of making a character judgment. For example, "You are lazy" or "You're just not trying" are character insults. These insults quickly create negative feedback loops that are hard to turn around. Instead, stick to the specifics of the performance. "These are the results we need to see, and this is where you are not meeting expectations." This framework applies whether it is an employee / direct report relationship, a business partner, or an executive. Keep the focus on the specifics, and refrain from making inferences about the person's character.

In Parts I through III, we discussed principles of human interactions that apply to most situations. In Part IV, you will learn techniques for dealing with Difficult People, those for whom normal rules of interaction do not apply. Difficult People make us doubt ourselves, and we waste time, energy, and money when we do not have sound strategies to cope with them. Worse, we make ourselves or our organizations vulnerable to litigation or other bad behavior. By identifying and interacting appropriately with Difficult People, you will learn how to protect your time and energy against toxic drains.

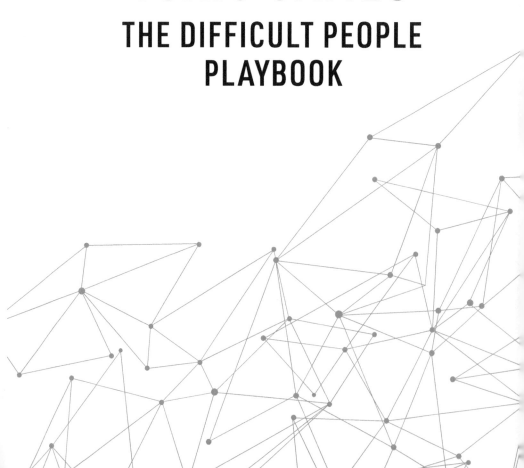

Part IV

TOXIC GAMES
THE DIFFICULT PEOPLE PLAYBOOK

Chapter 11

DIFFICULT PEOPLE
ARE PLAYING A
DIFFERENT GAME

n my office, I have a bookshelf. The topics center around leadership, productivity, and optimal functioning—the most frequent focus areas for my executive coaching clients. There is a book that doesn't belong. It is called the *Diagnostic and Statistical Manual of Mental Disorders* (*DSM*), and it contains the diagnoses and criteria that psychologists need to know for mental health diagnoses. While most psychologists have one, I no longer work with mental health diagnoses. So why is this book there?

Several times per year, the following conversation happens.

Client: "Tricia, this colleague is *crazy*." (Client proceeds to give me numerous examples to support the crazy diagnosis.)

"I've had many conversations with him, and I just can't get through."

Tricia: "What kind of conversations have you had?"

Client: "I tried to talk to him the way I would want someone to speak with me. I laid everything out in a logical manner to help him understand. I thought we were on the same page, but then he went to HR and complained that I was bullying him."

Tricia: "Rewind. You said he was crazy and irrational. Why would he respond to a rational dialogue?"

After my client discusses several ways in which he might be able to change the colleague's behavior, I get the *DSM*, open it up to a page under personality disorders, and show him why his efforts are fruitless. I need my client to understand that he is dealing with an irrational person and that an irrational person plays a different game.

Difficult People, those who are often irrational, lie on a continuum. Some have diagnosable personality disorders; others simply make your life more difficult. People with personality disorders cannot adapt relationally, and this inflexibility interferes with optimal personal and professional functioning. They have the same needs we discussed in chapter 8, but they try to fulfill them the wrong way. The degree to which the personality disorder interferes with daily functioning varies across individuals. They have families, hold jobs, and may be very intelligent. They are not irrational all the time. Thus, it is easy to assume that their behavior is associated with the situation. If you are untrained in psychology and you research personality disorders online, you may conclude that all of the people you dislike have diagnoses, which is unlikely to be true.

Because of the diagnostic complexity of personality disorders, I've broadened the conversation to "Difficult People." I show clients the DSM to let them know that personality disorders are "a real thing." But whether or not Difficult People have personality disorders, they all have significant personality deviations. Because they do not follow standard relationship rules, you need to approach them differently. If you interact with them like everyone else, you will lose. They are playing a different game.

PRE-GAME REQUIREMENTS

To effectively deal with Difficult People, we need to label them as "difficult" and adjust our game accordingly. Over the years, I have learned that high achievers struggle with these prerequisites because:

1.   High achievers value kindness, and labeling someone as "difficult" feels mean.

2.   High achievers want to maintain a rational game.

Feeling Mean

Tricia: "What's the 'but'?"

Client: "What do you mean?"

Tricia: "You agree with the information, but you are hesitating. What is the 'but'?"

Client: "If I acknowledge that this person is unlikely to change, it feels like I am throwing her away."

My clients are not the only ones who have difficulty placing people in categories. The discussion is a hard one for me to have, considering that, a few chapters ago, I talked about love, acceptance, and reaching into marshmallows. I, and most of my clients, value kindness, tolerance, and generosity. At the same time, we value peace of mind, self-respect, and self-preservation. Protecting ourselves from Difficult People means that we need to be less inclusive, less tolerant, and less forgiving. Herein lies the tension: how do we protect ourselves from Difficult People without sacrificing our value system? If we do not address that tension, we will continue to treat Difficult People as we do everyone else. This strategy perpetuates the problem. I had to figure it out the hard way.

When I was young, someone in my life bullied me. The person told me regularly that she hated my clothing, my choices, and my opinions. My interpretation of the Judeo-Christian faith with which I was raised was that if I wanted to be like Jesus, I needed to be kind, regardless of how others treated me. This approach made the situation worse. (Difficult People often perceive kindness as a weakness—more on that later.) At some point, I realized that my strategy wasn't working. I began standing up for myself. I wasn't mean; I simply stopped being passive. I started making statements like "You may think that my clothing is ugly, but I like it." "That is your opinion, and you have a right to it, but I disagree." Her behavior began to change.

The same pattern repeated itself with a colleague when I was a teenager in my first job. A colleague created power by removing her approval for those she disrespected (relational bullying). She was fun, friendly, and helpful to the people she liked; she was cold, dismissive, and unpleasant to those she disliked. Nobody wanted to displease her. My preferred mode of interaction is a happy collaboration where everybody wins. I was kind and helpful to my difficult colleague. I tried to engage her in conversation and make her feel special. I didn't over-apologize or "try too hard," yet I thought that basic civility might work.

Civility and kindness did not work. After about a month of that strategy, I was tired of trying. I decided to stop the effort. I spoke to my colleague only to accomplish the work tasks. My answers to her were short and unadorned. If we passed in the hall, I barely acknowledged her. I played her game. At the end of two weeks, her actions toward me changed. She was warmer, more talkative, and more helpful. Suddenly, she approved of me.

I worked there for several years, and she "liked me" for the remainder of my employment. At my going-away party, she gave me what she believed was a compliment. "You've changed so much since you first came." I thought, *No, I haven't changed at all. I just played your game.* During that experience, I never took her approval seriously. I never trusted her. I knew that her endorsement of me was not about me at all. Instead, she had a twisted value system about the kind of person she respected, and I played to that system.

Despite playing the game, I never compromised my integrity. I remained honest. I was not mean. I simply withdrew the openness, warmth, and transparency that I value. If I had not recognized my colleague as belonging to a different category, I would have continued addressing her from my perspective and endured four years of cold disapproval.

When we value people, we hesitate to put them into a Difficult People category. Making a judgment about someone and putting them into a box offends our sensibilities. It makes us feel mean. We may feel like we are violating a deeply held belief system or a personal moral code.

What if we can value Difficult People's humanity while drawing boundaries around their ability to create chaos? What if we can maintain our goodwill toward others but make wise decisions about whom we accept into our organizations or personal relationships? The dichotomous view of dealing with people suggests that people are all bad or all good, that we need to love everyone and accept them in all situations, or else we are hypocritical. Sometimes recognizing Difficult People and adjusting our expectations allows us to have more compassion than if we continue to expect them to be like everyone else.

Approaching Irrational People with a Rational Strategy

If someone looks and acts normal, we assume that they are rational. If you are a high achiever, you use logical reasoning and expect others to do the same. When they don't, you wonder if you are doing something wrong. As a high achiever, you think that if you could explain your position better, the other person would understand. You can't have a rational conversation with irrational people. If you continue to address the situation with your rational tool kit, you will fail.

Imagine that you go to a basketball game (Difficult Person's game), and you play by football rules (your game). You will lose, regardless of how good you are at football. While you would never apply football rules to basketball or Monopoly rules to chess, this is what you are doing when you use rational rules (football) for an irrational game (basketball). There are several reasons why we have difficulty adjusting to a different game:

1. Difficult People may be on a basketball court, but they will tell you that they are playing football. You like to think the best of people, so you believe them.

2. You don't want to play by basketball rules. Football is familiar and comfortable. You want to play your way, only harder.

3. Occasionally, Difficult People mix in football rules, and you doubt your judgment that they are playing basketball.

The best way to excel in identifying Difficult People and changing your game is to familiarize yourself with the red flags and then adjust your behavior accordingly.

RED FLAGS THAT SOMEONE IS PLAYING A DIFFERENT GAME

"It's funny. I saw red flags in the beginning. I thought that I could somehow change it. It reminds me of dating—when people notice the problems but think they can make it work. I learned not to do that in dating, but apparently, I am still doing it in business."
—A business owner who broke up
with her business partner

Below is a list of the most common red flags. Like the person above learned, they will only help you if you take them seriously. There are three rules you want to remember as you go through the red flag list:

1. Difficult People will not have all of the flags.

2. The presence of any flag is a problem.

3. The flags are not situation-specific or person-specific. Instead, you will notice a pattern of behavior across people and situations.

Red Flags Master List

1. They somehow make you feel crazy while simultaneously causing you to question yourself. "Is it me, or is it them?"

2. They seem to twist all conversations to mean something different. You see them doing this both with you and with other people.

3. They are unpredictable in their reactions. The same stimulus will elicit a different response, depending on the day. The only predictable thing is their unpredictability.

4. They lack close, long-standing relationships. Even introverts have one or two close friends whom they have known for a long time. Difficult People may make friends easily, but they cannot sustain the relationships. In professional situations, you may note a higher-than-usual amount of job-hopping. Across contexts, if you ask them about the demise of a job or friendship, it is always the other person's fault.

5. They are unable to take responsibility for their behavior.

6. They are easily offended. You always feel like you are walking on eggshells.

7. They are unable to put themselves in someone else's shoes. Their words or actions show no awareness of the other person's feelings, situation, or needs. You find yourself saying, "I would *never* say/do that to another person. What were they thinking?"

8. They are smooth talkers. Everything they say sounds good, but something feels wrong. You doubt your perception.

9. They seem to thrive on drama. Either their own life is in upheaval or someone else's is. They may intentionally

instigate problems where none exists (e.g., extrapolating statements from an innocent conversation and making it into a rumor that causes conflict and division).

10. They gossip about other people. They may make you feel special by including you as a confidante.

11. They tell you that you are the first fabulous person they have ever met. In this discussion, they disparage all of their past friends, bosses, or colleagues and somehow make you feel superior because you are different than all of the other dumb schmucks that have gone before you.

12. They need attention all the time. All the time. All the time. It...is...exhausting.

13. They have no boundaries. They divulge personal information too quickly. They regularly cross the line of what is appropriate.

14. They love compliments. They have to be the best. (We all do, right?) *But* they need ego stroking from their relationships. If you dare to criticize them, they will turn on you.

15. They show no gratitude. They believe the world owes them.

16. You dread conversations with them. If the conversation is more than 10 minutes, you feel exhausted. If the

conversation is 45 minutes, it seems to use up your
emotional reserves for the rest of the day.

17. They make you feel bad about yourself. They may do this
overtly, with blatant insults and put-downs. They may also
use the covert method of adding veiled insults, ignoring
you, or otherwise marginalizing your worth. Either way,
their approach makes it difficult for you to fight back.

18. Other people are afraid of them.

19. They make you feel like you are on an emotional roller
coaster. They may love you one day and hate you the next.

20. They say things that put you on the defensive and make
you want to respond. Examples: "Oh, so you don't care
about me, do you?" "You lied about what you promised
me. I thought your company had integrity." "You think
I'm stupid, don't you?" The comments undermine your
character or one of your core values.

21. They threaten to sue people over trivial matters.

22. They align themselves with one other person, but this
alignment changes. The previous friend can become the
enemy, with no respect for the first relationship.

23. They don't take no for an answer.

24. They are always the victim.

25. They are negative. They are unable to recount their situation or listen to someone else's and celebrate the good. They highlight the negative and shade the positive with ugly foreboding, "Well, I had a good day, but you know that never lasts long."

26. They set no boundaries for their self-care and then make you feel bad for daring to have your own. Think "martyr."

27. You always feel like they are trying to pull something out of you, but you're unsure what it is.

28. They are easily offended, even when you are as kind and supportive as possible.

29. They take any type of "no" as a personal rejection.

30. They use guilt trips when you attempt to set a boundary.

31. They use silent treatment / removal of approval to coerce others into bending to their wishes.

What to Do When You See Red Flags

Our red flag recognition is worthless if we do not use the warning signs to alter our behavior. You can protect yourself by creating a pause in your response and by holding your cards close.

The Pause—Protection and Due Diligence

Remember the pause? We can use the pause to get information, without acting on it right away. It is a protective strategy, and the higher the stakes, the longer the pause should be. People are vulnerable to violating the pause when they simply want to get a decision out of the way. For example, if you are tired of interviewing, you may ignore the red flag if the candidate seems competent.

In high-stakes situations, we need to pause until we have all of the information and an airtight case. In one high-stakes situation, it was quickly apparent that my opposition would not respond to conversation, script changes, or compassion. Two of my experienced colleagues said, "Tricia, you don't want to go up against them. You are walking into a snake pit." I paused. I listened. I gathered information until everything was dotted and crossed. I walked into the snake pit. I won.

When we wait until we have all of the information, we no longer need to rely on our own opinion. We do not have to waste energy making an argument or defending ourselves. The pause has given us all of the resources we need, and our silence leaves the enemy uncertain of our position. Sun Tzu, the military strategist, noted in his book *The Art of War* that "every battle is lost or won before it is ever fought." Pausing keeps us from showing our cards and entering the battle prematurely. When we pause and hold our cards close, we can optimize the outcome before we engage.

Hold Your Cards Close

I frequently use the phrase "hold your cards close." The idiom comes from card games, in which a player holds his or her cards close to the chest so that other players do not see them. Difficult People are adept at getting us to show our cards. They push our buttons to elicit a reaction. Whether we show our emotions or engage verbally, we give them information that they can use against us. We make ourselves targets when we react without knowing the game that the other person is playing.

If you are innately honest or want people to like you, you will likely overexplain and show your cards. In high-trust relationships, reactions are optimal. It's part of transparency, honesty, and highly engaging dialogues. I react a lot with my clients and close friends because I know who they are. I don't need to "hold my cards close," because I already figured out that we are playing the same game.

When you get to know someone, reveal less at the onset, especially in situations with high-stakes potential. We show our cards through our words, lack of words, tone of voice, and facial expression. To some extent, we can't control what we reveal, especially the micro-expressions that we discussed earlier. Emotionally intuitive people may see things we don't want them to see. You will protect yourself if you develop a pleasantly neutral expression that you can use when assessing the other players at the beginning of the game. Pausing and holding one's cards close creates the space for us to choose effective basketball strategies while keeping our integrity intact.

BASKETBALL PLAYS FOR ALL DIFFICULT PEOPLE

Kusushi

"*Kusushi*" is a martial-arts term that means "breaking balance." The strategies involve throwing opponents off-balance. Throwing opponents off-balance is second only to keeping your cards close when it comes to effective techniques for dealing with Difficult People. Earlier, we discussed that humans automatically have scripts for what is supposed to happen in a situation. If I insult you, I expect you to get offended or insult me back. Imagine for a moment that you insult someone, and he or she starts singing "Happy Birthday" to you.

Whenever we add a twist to an expected script, we throw someone off-balance. There are a few ways to do this. We can use the opponent's momentum against him, cut off the oxygen source, or erratically change the script.

Using People's Momentum against Them

Using someone else's momentum to disrupt balance is a common component of both judo and jujutsu. Here is my layperson's understanding of the concept. Suppose that someone runs at you full-force. If you step aside, they run into the wall. If you fight back, you unwittingly provide a cushion that may be less effective than letting them run into the wall. Plus, you might get injured in the process. Please note that there is *nothing* passive about letting someone run into a wall. One of my friends and I had a recurring "argument" on this strategy because she hears "stepping aside" as "being a doormat." This strategy intends to hurt your opponent in a way that maintains your integrity while decreasing future bad behavior. The first way to use people's momentum against them is agreement.

Agreement

Every person who wants to fight is putting a lot of energy into the game. If you twist that energy, you win. The best way to do this is to agree. (My authentic people: I am going to tell you to be disingenuous. I'm sorry. I promise integrity, but overdisclosure is not an option with Difficult People.)

Difficult Person: "You only care about the money!"

Me: "You're right. I do care about the money."

Difficult Person: "You just don't know what you are talking about."

Me: "You could be right."

Rationale: Agreement uses the other person's momentum against them. The above scripts show that you know what he or she is trying to do and are just refusing to play. There is nowhere left to go in the conversation.

The Difficult Person will likely escalate and make more accusations. You want to agree with them. If agreement makes you feel like you are lying, opt for something like "Okay," as used in the example below.

Difficult Person: "You're a liar!"

Me: "Okay."

If this conversation is happening with a room full of people, you can be kind, gracious, and agreeable the whole time. The Difficult

Person is figuratively running herself into the wall, with a lot of witnesses. She will generally cease when she realizes it. If she doesn't, you will look incredibly sane by comparison.

The key to making this strategy work is to **maintain the agreement throughout the escalation.** I've role-played being a Difficult Person with my clients. By the fifth or sixth accusation, they break character and start defending themselves. When you break down and explain, you give away more power and worsen the situation. You show the Difficult Person how to push your buttons. The only successful solution allows the person to run into a wall until he or she gives up.

Allowing people to run themselves into the wall gives us power. It shows that we do not have to defend ourselves. It also shows that we have no cracks in our armor. Thus, Difficult People understand that they will only hurt themselves by playing the game with us. If we have confidence, aren't willing to play the game, and may even have a game of our own, they won't try to play. After you practice Difficult People games long enough, you won't have to deal with Difficult People nearly as often. You will be able to identify them and keep them at a distance, or they will sense that you are more powerful and will move on to an easier target.

Take Statements at Face Value—Disregard Subtext

Using people's momentum against them by agreeing is one form of *Kusushi*. Another way to throw a person off-balance is to respond to their statement's literal meaning rather than the intended meaning. The people who excel at emotional jabs do so with subtle innuendo that makes you want to fight but leaves you feeling defenseless.

Difficult Person: "You're probably too busy to help me with this today."

(**Intention:** I want your help, but I don't want to ask, so I'm going to involve you in a ridiculous game through which I want you to offer to help against your will, but then it's you who offered in the first place such that it can't be my fault. I will use the emotional manipulation of guilt to achieve my goal.)

You: "You're right! I *am* super-busy. I appreciate you recognizing that. If you still need help next week, feel free to email me."

By taking the initial statement at face value, you don't reinforce the Difficult Person's unhealthy strategy. You also gave a compliment, which makes it difficult for her to be upset. Further, you have offered to help, but you put the onus on her to check back with you next week.

Together, this means that you are setting a precedent that:

1. Indirect requests will not be rewarded.

2. You will not accommodate someone else's vague crisis.

3. You are not a good target for emotional manipulation.

Another example of choosing a literal interpretation:

Difficult Person: "Wow, it's great that you get to leave work early. I'm dedicated to my job, so I usually stay late."

You: "You're right! I feel blessed to leave early. And I can tell that you're dedicated. I hope you have a great evening!"

Game-Stopping Statements

Over the years, I have used two statements to effectively shock Difficult People and shut down the game before it even starts. I mentioned one earlier.

If someone tries to make me feel guilty for stating a need, opinion, or stance, I say:

1. "Yeah…I'm impervious to guilt trips, so you're going to have to try harder."

2. "Just to be clear, you're trying to make me feel bad about this? You suck at it. Try harder."

Depending on the situation, I can deliver the lines playfully, with intensity, or with complete neutrality. The words are strong enough such that I can use a little verbal/nonverbal incongruence and the message still comes through. If the person is difficult, it tells him or her that I recognize the game. If the person was playful and I had an overreaction, that person understands the boundaries. I'm kind in the moments before and after the statement. The point isn't to engage conflict; it's to stop it before it has a chance to develop.

Have I ever alienated someone by overreacting with a game-stopping statement? Maybe. But, honestly, none of the great people in my life use social manipulation or peer pressure as an opening joke in the "getting to know you" stage. I'm all about busting someone's chops in a safe relationship, but if a person does that at the onset of engagement, it sends a message of game-playing, insecurity, or poor judgment.

Game-stopping statements work best in social settings where there is little consequence. In work settings, Difficult People could twist your words and use them against you. Taking comments at face value is a better strategy for work settings because you are simply responding to a Difficult Person's statement rather than making one of your own.

Strategic Nonengagement

Agreement, disregarding subtext, and game-stopping statements are forms of throwing people off-balance and not engaging in their game. Strategic nonengagement can be useful when you need to pull a power play, shut off the oxygen, or discontinue someone's behavior.

First, nonengagement means that you don't respond. At all.

When people are pulling for a reaction, and you give them none, you send the message "I'm so confident that I don't need to respond." Nonengagement is *not* recommended for bullies, because the bully may incorrectly read it as a weakness.

Nonengagement removes oxygen from people who thrive on drama. Difficult People often want to pull something from us. They have a hidden agenda. When we react, we fuel that agenda.

Disengaging from people and limiting contact makes it difficult for them to push our buttons, steal our oxygen, and otherwise draw us into their toxic vortex.

Nonengagement ends participation. Obvious? Read on. If you no longer want to interact with a person or discuss a specific topic, stop responding. I've had many women ask me how to get a person to stop texting. Simple answer: stop responding. Assuming that you have already said, "I am not interested in continuing our friendship. I wish you well," the next and final step is silence.

Arguments:
"But, Tricia, I don't want to be rude."
"Maybe if I just stay cordial and polite, he'll get the message."
"But, Tricia, I feel like I just need to let this person know where the boundaries lie."

When people want a response, any response is reinforcing and continues the engagement. Being kind rewards them. Arguing encourages them. Asking them to stop reinforces them. In simple scenarios, they perceive the response as an open door to keep pushing. In higher-stakes scenarios, you show more of your cards than you can imagine, thus making you vulnerable.

Distraction and Redirection

Imagine that you land in an arena with a bull who appears intent on charging you. What happens? People may scream at the bull. A clown may jump out to grab the bull's attention. You may run back and forth, switching directions rapidly so that you are a moving target instead of a sitting duck. What do all of these techniques have in common? They rely on distraction. People who understand bull behavior will be best prepared to understand what is most likely to distract the bull. Distracting the bull gives you time to escape and may cause him to forget that he was about to charge you in the first place.

If you would like to waste your time effectively, fight the bull. If you are protective of your time, distracting Difficult People from their intention can save you a lot of unwanted energy. Human self-absorption is a great asset. It's easy to distract people by getting them to talk about themselves.

The best points of distraction are passion points. Sometimes I got tired of taking notes in college. I didn't want to miss any information because I wanted a good grade. I also needed a break from paying attention. My strategy was to figure out a professor's hobby or pet peeve. Then I asked questions that linked the passion point to the topic at hand to make the query appear relevant. I knew that the passion point would take the teacher on an irresistible tangent. Twenty minutes of a brain break—done.

You can derail everyone from their topic. The passion points are their kids, sports teams, politics, egos, clothing, or a different worry that makes you look empathetic but keeps you disengaged from the real topic. Learning how to use distraction allows you to give short replies, no replies, or non-answers. You can appear agreeable while casually dancing away from the topic. (Non-answers sound like an answer, but they don't give any information. We will discuss them in the next section.)

Non-answers and Ridiculous Answers

One of my favorite landmark psychological studies addressed people's responses to different forms of requests. Ellen Lang conducted the study in 1978 when copying machines were used as a way of replicating information.[1]

In the study, the researcher asked to cut in front of people waiting to make copies. The researcher asked to cut in line in one of three ways:

1. "Excuse me, I have five pages. May I use the Xerox machine?" (No reason)

2. "Excuse me, I have five pages. May I use the Xerox machine *because* I'm in a rush?" ("Because" with reason)

3. "Excuse me, I have five pages. May I use the Xerox machine *because* I have to make copies?" ("Because" with no reason)

When the researcher used "because," as noted in statements 2 and 3, a significantly higher number of people allowed the line cutting. They acquiesced to the request regardless of the words that followed "because." This study, on non-reasons, formed the foundation for my use and recommendation of "non-answers."

---

1   Ellen Land, "The Mindlessness of Ostensibly Thoughtful Action: The Role of 'Placebic' Information in Interpersonal Interaction," *Journal of Personality and Social Psychology* 36, no. 6 (1978): 635–642.

As reasonable people, we want to make statements and requests that are logical and credible. This assumption is a good one in relationships with rational people, but it oxygenates irrational people's arguments. Hence, using non-answers can pacify without making you vulnerable to their games. A non-answer works exceptionally well when you follow it with a distracting question.

> *Difficult Person:* "Why don't you want to volunteer?"
> *Me:* "Because I don't volunteer." (Uses "because")

> *Difficult Person:* "Why won't you answer me?"
> *Me:* "Because that's the way I roll." (Uses "because")

> *Difficult Person:* "Do you think it's fair that Sally got a promotion?"
> *Me:* "I don't know. I don't know what I think about promotions." (Without "because")

After any non-answers, follow with a distracting question, preferably an ego-stroking one.

> *"...That's just the way I roll. By the way, I noticed that you did a great job with that project last week. How did you do it?"*

A variation on the non-answer is the ridiculous one. Here are some examples of ridiculous answers using the same questions.

> *Difficult Person:* "Why won't you answer me?"

Me: "When I was a kid, my friend was a snowman. I learned that conversation doesn't make a lot of sense."

Difficult Person: "Do you think it's fair that Sally got a promotion?"

Me: "Huh. I don't know. I think she has great hair."

Ridiculous answers have one purpose only—to make Difficult People go away. Of course, you will use your judgment about the situations in which they are appropriate. Here is an inside piece of information, though, that will allow you to scale the ridiculousness and use it even when you need to appear intelligent and competent.

**People always assume that there
is a reason for what we say.**

If you can make a ridiculous statement or ask a nonsensical question while keeping your face and body language serious, they will spin for hours, trying to figure out what you meant. By itself, this is a power play that will make Difficult People less likely to engage with you.

KEY TAKEAWAYS

1. *If you are a nice person, you will feel mean when you first deal effectively with Difficult People.*

2. *You can't have a rational conversation with an irrational person.*

3. *If you play the game using the rules that feel comfortable to you, you will lose.*

LEADERSHIP APPLICATION

1. Transparent leadership tactics do not apply to Difficult People. Watch and listen without revealing your cards.

2. If you have someone in your professional arena with several red flags, begin documenting the problems and pay attention to the specific plays in the next chapter.

Chapter 12

SPECIFIC PLAYS FOR CATEGORIES OF DIFFICULT PEOPLE

EGGSHELL ETHEL

Description

She is named Eggshell Ethel because you always feel like you're walking on eggshells. She thinks you are the best thing since sliced bread one day and the spawn of Satan the next. The problem is that you have no idea what you did within that 24-hour period that caused the switch. Eggshell Ethel gets easily offended and holds grudges forever. She twists the words that you say. If you apologize, Eggshell Ethel will use that apology to fuel her fire. If you attempt to hold her accountable, she will lash out at you in a rage. There is no such thing as a straightforward, honest conversation with Eggshell Ethel. She will use all of the information you give and turn it against you.

In its milder form, Eggshell Ethel will be a frustrating time suck. You will always have to watch your words, mask your reactions, and give her the most positive feedback you can. If you say anything remotely constructive, you need to wrap it in the thickest blanket of sugar imaginable, and honestly, you still won't win.

In her more severe form, Eggshell Ethel is a threat to you and your company. She will sue you. Eggshell Ethel may threaten to hurt herself, you, or others. The only thing you can predict from Eggshell Ethel is that she will be wholly irrational most of the time.

How do you have compassion for Eggshell Ethel while placing her in the Difficult People category? Eggshell Ethel is desperate for love and real relationships. Rejection is death for her. She does not have the knowledge, strength, and wherewithal to change her approach to people. It is not your job to be involved with her, as she would need professional assistance to change. You can still send good thoughts or prayers her way as she is likely to remain stuck in a vortex of loneliness and pain.

Optimal Strategy

Get as far away from Eggshell Ethel as you can. If she is a family member or a social acquaintance, limit your interactions. Do not give Eggshell Ethel access to your social media accounts. If access is unavoidable, screen all of your postings through the lens of the way Eggshell Ethel might use it.

If you are an organizational leader, ensure that you have a hiring process to screen out potential Eggshell Ethels. If Eggshell Ethel is already in your organization, you need to quarantine her influence under the guise of doing her a favor (think a fake promotion to an island in the ocean). Document interactions to cover your butt.

Specific Strategies for When You Must Interact

1. **Don't believe anything she says.** Don't assume that anything is rational. Don't engage. Whether she runs at you with a compliment or an insult, just smile politely and step aside.

2. **Ensure that you don't respond to her innuendos.** She designs them to put you on the defensive and convince you to share more than you had intended. Take statements at face value, even if you understand the

innuendo. Respond to the literal statement rather than the subtext.

3. **Develop self-talk to get you through the emotional manipulation.** "It's not about me. She is playing her game. It's not about me."

It's incredibly difficult not to react when someone is pushing all of your buttons. It helps to understand what they are doing and that it's not personal. I remember one appointment in which Eggshell Ethel pressed my buttons nonstop with her innuendos and insults. I was angry for an hour, and I needed to pretend the whole time that I wasn't. I couldn't fire her when I wanted because Eggshell Ethels are sensitive to rejection and pose a litigation risk. What got me through was this self-talk: "You know what she's doing, Tricia; you can't give her the reaction. You just need to stay calm until you can get her out." I said this to myself over and over. I'm sure it shortened to a mantra of "Don't react. Don't react. Don't react."

What the nonreaction gets you: Eggshell Ethel will eventually understand that she is slamming into a brick wall. Along the way, she may cry, fight, or increase the pressure. If you have been engaging with her and shift to nonreactive tactics, there will be a period where she will intensify the pressure in an attempt to push you back into position. Eventually, she will give up. Once you've mastered the game of basketball, you'll automatically set precedents that discourage manipulation. These nonverbal messages will cause the Eggshell Ethels to ignore you and seek out more rewarding targets.

BLIND BILLY

Description

As I describe Billy, you may quickly recognize him as having a personality style that people refer to as narcissistic. Many people correlate narcissism to being "full of oneself" or "egotistical." However, the salient characteristic that can be hard to understand is that Billy is also blind, blind to you and everyone else. Blind Billys are self-absorbed. Some Blind Billys are harmless; others are destructive.

Blind Billy has no idea about the way he or she impacts others. He may not care. I often hear a client say, "If he would just put himself in my shoes..." This is a fatal mistake because Blind Billy does not recognize that you are a different person than him, let alone the fact that you wear shoes. Expecting him to understand that you wear sneakers while he wears loafers is a waste of your time.

Did you ever get presents from people who gave you *their* favorite things, even though you have opposite tastes? Blind Billy coalesces his needs and yours. There is no "me" versus "you" because he does not view the two of you as separate entities.

Blind Billy needs other people to recognize how important he is. We all want to feel special, but you'll note that Blind Billy perks up immensely when he receives affirmation of his greatness. Early in my professional career, I found myself sitting in the office of a CEO. Numerous people had told me that he was a Blind Billy and that the path to his heart was to stroke his ego. CEO Blind Billy and an attorney pressed me to go against my ethics to further a frivolous legal agenda. It was a matter of integrity for me, so I refused. The attorney threatened to show up the next morning with a subpoena or possibly a court order to convince me.

With tears streaming down my face, I looked at Blind Billy, CEO, and said, "Sir, I know that you are a man of integrity and that you care about this company." I watched his torso shift as he sat up straight. His chest puffed out, and he breathed deeply. They dismissed me a few minutes later. A few hours later, my colleague told me that the matter had been dropped. She said, "The attorney wanted to apologize to you for being a bitch." The next morning, another leader of the company walked into my office and said, "I heard you stood your ground. That's cool." We can maintain our integrity when playing a different game, but we need to know who we are playing against to use the right rules.

Besides the high need for ego-stroking, you can recognize Blind Billy by his complete lack of attention when other people are talking. I recall a supervisor who animatedly spoke about his weekend. Then he turned to me and said, "How was your weekend?" I said three words, and his eyes glazed over. Blind Billy can follow social protocols of reciprocity, but if you watch his eyes and affect, you'll notice a decided lack of engagement when the attention is not on him. Like all personality characteristics, the desire for ego-stroking and attention in itself is not the flag. Rather, it is the degree to which a person requires it in every interaction that separates a Blind Billy from people who simply want to be seen and heard.

Blind Billy cannot take criticism. Never, ever criticize a Blind Billy. At best, your complaint will simply fall on deaf ears. More frequently, Blind Billy will become angry by your criticism. He will either attack you directly or cut you off emotionally. Blind Billy is unlikely to take responsibility for failures. Thus, even a straightforward conversation about what went wrong will be a dead end.

Blind Billy appreciates you to the extent that you can do something for him. He will give precedent to people of higher status because those associations boost his image. Blind Billy may be friendly to you, but understand that the relationship will only last as long as you have something he values.

Blind Billy's need for external validation means that he will always play to the audience in front of him. The observer will wonder why he lies or contradicts himself across situations. He may be unaware of doing so. Many of us have a sense of being a hypocrite if we are incongruent. Blind Billy does not have this level of awareness. Instead, he is actively engaged in looking smart, prestigious, and powerful to the audience in front of him. He will say or do whatever he believes will further his status.

How do you have compassion for Blind Billy while also placing him in the Difficult People category? Blind Billy has no internal sense of who he is. His entire sense of self rests on the fragile facade of how he presents to others. While Blind Billy seems to overflow with self-worth, he has no self-worth. Because of this, he is unlikely to have a depth of purpose or sustain deep, meaningful relationships.

Optimal Strategy

Keep Blind Billy in the acquaintance zone of relationships. You want to be friendly, likable, and polite. If Blind Billy is at your workplace, keep the conversation focused on work and throw in occasional ego strokes. Blind Billy may be a nice guy, but do not expect Blind Billy to recognize your hard work or your needs. Do not expect Blind Billy to advocate on your behalf unless it makes him look good. Do not expect Blind Billy to be loyal to you. You want to stay in Blind Billy's favor while holding him at arm's length. This strategy will allow you the maximum amount of autonomy. If you need something from Blind Billy, always present an argument that shows how it will raise his status.

Specific Strategies for When You Must Interact

1. Do not "try to make him understand." Focus on the facts of the situation and how fabulous he is.

2. Ego-stroke to get what you want. Make everything look according to his benefit.

3. If Blind Billy wants something from you and you have to say no, ego-stroke excessively.

4. Invent questions so that you can ask Blind Billy for his opinions or advice.

5. Never lose sight of the fact that your value to him depends on your utility to him.

6. You are in control of the game, but you need him to think that he is.

7. Do not ever engage in a power struggle. Remember that he is right.

ENTITLED EDDIE (OR OUTRAGED OLIVER?)

Description

Entitled Eddie thinks that everyone owes him. Entitled Eddie will flummox you because you expect him to be grateful, but he will only criticize you for whatever you did not give him. You see, you cannot get to a zero balance with Eddie, because whatever you give is never enough. Eddie never owes anyone else because he deserves everything in the first place.

I once had an Entitled Eddie call me for business coaching. He complained that the economy had changed and that no one valued his expertise. He complained that people were not willing to pay him what he was worth. He told me that he was excellent—fantastic, in fact—and in the top 1% of his industry. Going with my gut, I looked up his website. In the frequently asked questions section, his information about fees was this: "I am an excellent (name of occupation), and I expect to get paid accordingly." He had no evidence to support his excellence. I knew that he would be unable to hear that his lack of sales was due to his personality. Fortunately, I was too expensive for him, which made him want to opt out of services (of course, he asked for a discount).

I have not specified this Entitled Eddie's occupation, because I do not know if he has Outraged Oliver characteristics. I am protecting myself if he reads this book. Entitled Eddies are annoying; Outraged Olivers are dangerous. Some Entitled Eddies became Outraged Olivers when you fail to see how special they are. While Entitled Eddies are merely frustrating, Outraged Olivers often seek retribution when you upset them. These people are litigation risks.

At one point in my career, I worked as an administrator at a university. One student had a reputation for creating waves. He was a jerk to the professors and then complained that the professors discriminated against him. He threatened lawsuits and had engaged in one at a previous institution. Everyone involved, including myself, had one agenda—ego-stroke him to graduation or until he changed schools. Someone said, "We are collectively holding our breath until he is out."

In some cases, dealing with Outraged Olivers may create ethical challenges. For example, a university has an ethical responsibility to ensure that people who graduate have met the minimum criteria for their specialty. In work situations, ego-stroking the person who misbehaves can induce bad workplace morale. Imagine a family where the irritating kid gets all of the attention, and the well-behaved kid is ignored. In both families and organizations, this approach decreases everyone's performance.

Whether you are in a business, a church organization, or a university, get a reliable legal team to handle Outraged Olivers and other Difficult People who are litigation risks. Legal support not only protects your organization, but their presence can give you the confidence to make the calls that are best for others on the team. You can save money on legal fees by solidly screening potential job candidates for personality issues or character flaws. A multi-person interview team, an outside psychologist, or even some specific interview questions can help you keep the Entitled Eddies and Outraged Olivers out of the organization. (See *www.relationalgenius.com* for additional resources.)

Optimal Strategy

First, you need to ascertain whether Entitled Eddie is annoying and harmless or if he has Outraged Oliver characteristics. Outraged Oliver shows up as extreme anger when he does not get his wishes. This person is a litigation risk.

If you are simply dealing with Entitled Eddie, set a boundary and do not move from it. The only way that he will stop expecting more is for you to stop giving him more. He will push harder for a while. Ignore the complaints, victim-speak, or guilt trips; hold firm. If your Entitled Eddie has Outraged Oliver characteristics, ego-stroke him the whole way out the door.

How do you find compassion for Entitled Eddie / Outraged Oliver? People universally dislike Entitled Eddie, and he is unlikely to have positive relationships. Further, because he cannot take responsibility, he will always have a ceiling on how far he can get in life.

Specific Strategies for When You Must Interact

1. Do not offer anything. Whether it be of time, money, or grace, any gift will instantly set a precedent for what he thinks he deserves.

2. Set specific, concrete boundaries early and don't move them an inch. If you already moved the line, pull it back by saying, "I'm sorry, I gave the wrong impression." Apologies are helpful for ego-soothing, even if you haven't done anything wrong.

3. When he asks for more of anything, say that you'd love to, but you can't. Then instantly change the subject to his weekend or one of his recent successes.

4. Understand that the entitled person will not like you better or worse if you give more. You owe him no matter what you do, so if you play his game, you lose.

5. Use the word "can't." Repeatedly. "I can't give you that." If he asks you for a reason, don't provide the rationale. If you use the word "won't," you play into his schema that everyone is willfully withholding what he rightfully deserves. "Can't" suggests that something is outside of your control and reduces his reactivity.

6. If you are scared of losing this person from the organization because of his skillset, understand that he is toxic and that you are gambling with a loss of morale for everyone on the team.

7. If he has Outraged Oliver characteristics, and he is in your business, document everything. Make sure that HR

is aware that he may be a threat. The ultimate goal is to manage him out without getting sued. If you can ego-stroke him and make him think that leaving was his idea, you will win. "You're right; you do deserve so much more than what we can give you. Have you considered a job in X industry?" You may pay more than you want to get him out of the game. It's worth it.

8. Remember—he is incapable of gratitude or taking responsibility for his mistakes. Do not waste your time trying to create insight.

Differentiation Note: Entitled Eddie or Blind Billy? Entitled Eddie sees other people—he sees how they should serve him. He has an ongoing deficit in which people are not giving him enough. Blind Billy is self-absorbed, but he doesn't necessarily have the victim mentality that Entitled Eddie does. If you are dealing with someone who has characteristics of both Blind Billy and Entitled Eddie, your strategy is to ego-stroke, create distance, avoid criticism, and abstain from straightforward, rational conversations.

DRAMATIC DORY

Description

On the outside, Dramatic Dory looks a lot like Eggshell Ethel. Both of them take the tiniest emotional spark and wave it into a raging brushfire. Where they differ, however, is their level of predictability. Eggshell Ethel is notoriously unpredictable. You can safely assume that whenever you think she will zig, she will zag. If you say something that you intend as a compliment, she may take it as an insult. As we have discussed, Eggshell Ethel can also be a legal threat.

Dramatic Dory
© Dr. Tricia Groff

On the other hand, Dramatic Dory is entirely predictable and less likely to be a threat. You can predict that if she hears the tiniest seed for gossip, she will embellish it and quickly fan it into a full-spread rumor. At the same time, if someone in the office has an illness or a car accident, she may be one of the first to step up and organize a massive "take care of the coworker" party.

Dramatic Dory thrives on heightened emotion. Eggshell Ethel's emotional volcano relates to her own feelings; Dramatic Dory will amplify other people's emotions and use them as her own. It gives her a place in the world.

Dramatic Dory will take a simple conflict and portray it as a life-threatening brawl. A straightforward request is a monumental undertaking, and a small reprimand is the end of the world as we know it. Dramatic Dory thrives on drama, and if it doesn't exist, she will create it. If you say something even remotely negative about a colleague, she will exaggerate what you said and spread it to others.

Optimal Strategy

Drama requires oxygen. Attention is oxygen. If you don't want drama, don't give it attention. Would gossip exist if everyone refused to pass it on? Imagine a workplace culture in which Dramatic Dory used the dialogue in the cartoon above and everyone simply shrugged. She would not receive any positive reinforcement, and she would move on to a new topic. The optimal response is to give no attention to Dramatic Dory when she is dramatic. When she is acting like a sane, rational human being, praise her. Since Dramatic Dorys often need attention, you can manipulate this need to pull out the best in her. Reward her with attention when she is behaving well.

How do you have compassion for Dramatic Dory? She doesn't have the personal security to understand that she can get attention without using others' emotions or struggles. Additionally, she will likely place herself in situations that guarantee drama, creating a much harder life for herself.

© Dr. Tricia Groff

One of my clients put it this way: "Tricia, this woman, I'm sure she's the nicest lady. But she is one of those people who makes a wind sprint to catch the struggle bus to Struggle Town."

Specific Strategies for When You Must Interact

1. *Never* use emotional inflection with Dramatic Dory. Stick to essential details, and keep conversations short.

2. Be nonresponsive to Dory's drama, and teach the people around you how to do the same.

3. If you reprimand her for spreading gossip, document accordingly. Assume that she will throw a tantrum. Tell HR ahead of time. Reprimand her on Friday afternoon so that you can protect the team from the immediate aftermath.

4. Do not seek to explain things, either verbally or on text/email. Responsiveness fuels the drama.

5. Reinforce positive behaviors to Dory and the team. Work to develop a culture where drama and gossip are "uncool." You can do this by making comments in team meetings. "I appreciate the emotional maturity that I see in this team. I notice that _____ and _____ (call out people who are constructive and steady) are exceptionally good at addressing problems directly and finding solutions with minimal fuss.

NEGATIVE NELLY

Description

Negative Nelly isn't toxic such that she will willfully hurt you or the organization. She is difficult because she sucks the life out of you. Nelly never sees anything positive. She may criticize others and the organization or simply bemoan her sad life and continuous hardships. Either way, everyone focuses on placating her or making her feel better.

All of us have our periods of being negative and needing to vent. Healthy people can reel in the negative and add a positive spin. Negative Nellies do not have that capacity. I worked with a technically brilliant colleague who left me exhausted after each interaction. She was a self-aware Negative Nelly, and she put it this way: "Tricia, you know how on the airplanes, those oxygen masks come down? You're supposed to use your own first and then help other people with theirs. I don't have my own oxygen mask, so I feed off of other people's oxygen. I need their oxygen to survive." When she said that, I immediately thought, *That's it. No wonder I'm exhausted.*

Her insight didn't solve my exhaustion, but I have always respected her intelligence to so clearly conceptualize the problem.

If you have a sunny, optimistic personality, you will attract Negative Nellies. Your energy and kindness will often make them feel better in the moment. Negative Nellies are often the perpetrators of the emotional vomit we discussed earlier.

Optimal Strategy

Recognize that you are unlikely to make Negative Nelly see things from a positive perspective. Trying to do so will leave you drained and frustrated. It is better to work on adding a buffer that limits your exposure to her.

How do you have compassion for Negative Nelly? Recall that I suggested that you limit your exposure. This reaction is the one she garners from many people—that they want to keep their distance. It impedes her ability to build relationships or build a promising career, and she may never understand the reason.

Negative Nellies are usually not dangerous, so if this is someone you love, you may have a small opening to let her know that her negativity pushes people away. She will likely cry and get defensive, but there is a slim chance that she may take the insight and do better.

Specific Strategies for When You Must Interact

1. Do not ask Negative Nelly how she is doing. You don't have 45 minutes to listen to the answer.

2. If you must engage Negative Nelly because she is a close colleague or family member, always plan to have a

follow-up meeting, task, or other items so that you can limit the interaction time.

3. Reverse all of the nonverbals that you usually do to get people to open up. Specifically, do not nod, sustain eye contact, or use verbal encouragers (i.e., hmm, uh-uh). These signals encourage people to keep on talking.

4. Do not use verbal empathy. Saying "That must be so frustrating" encourages everyone to open up about their feelings. You don't want to do that with Negative Nelly.

5. When she demeans herself, don't argue. Nothing you say will make a difference. Instead, you might say something like, "I have some friends with similar feelings. They've found it helpful to see a counselor." You can show caring without being the person who is doing the caring.

6. Don't ask open-ended questions (What do you think? How do you feel?). Open-ended questions facilitate personal disclosure. You don't want Negative Nelly to talk more.

7. Change the subject to something positive at every opportunity. "That's an interesting point. Which reminds me, did you see X great movie this weekend?" Of course, Negative Nelly will find the negative aspects of each topic, but you can still control which topics you discuss.

8. If you are highly empathetic, go to the discussion on emotional vomit and look at the tips to protect you from Negative Nelly's energy.

TORMENTING TOM AND TYRANNICAL TANYA – BULLIES

Description

First, the reason for two mnemonics is because men and women often bully differently. Tom will tend to make verbal threats and actively take action to block your success. Tanya will tend to use relational intimidation—such as rolling her eyes or whispering behind your back so that you can hear. Both of them may make loaded comments that make you feel bad. Bullies are exceptionally good at finding a vulnerability or creating one and exploiting it to make you feel inferior.

We know the way bullies act and how they make us feel from our experience in elementary, middle, and high school. The ages may change; the dynamics do not. For that reason, I want to talk to you about some high school clients from one of my past professional lives.

Conversation:

Female High School Girl: "Tricia, all of the adults tell me to ignore it. Just walk away. I've tried that. It doesn't work."

Male High School Client: "You are telling me to push back. That is what my parents say too. I'm afraid of making it worse. I don't want to fight. I don't want to get in trouble."

Stupid Advice

Stupid Advice #1: Don't Let Them Get to You

First, the bully is fabulous at "getting to people." They can smell your weak spots, your vulnerability, and your values. They know every soft spot and how to twist the knife. Do you know how I could "get to" every woman in America right now? I would say, "You know, your thighs remind me of a pet elephant, but don't worry about them, because your ass casts a shadow over them" *or* I could give her a once-over with my eyes, slightly shake my head, and walk away. Relational bullying. Done. It doesn't matter what she does or doesn't say; I know that she will go home, stare in the mirror that night, and worry. I know that she will avoid me tomorrow because she fears what I will say next.

I wrote the above paragraph, which made me feel dirty, in two min-utes, just by knowing common sensitivities. Can you imagine what bullies can do with only a little more ammunition and the incentive to use it? We are human, and pretending that bullies shouldn't get to us:

1. is a fantasy; and

2. causes us to feel like a failure because we feel weak.
    This false perception of weakness makes it even more challenging to handle the bullies.

Stupid Advice #2: Just Walk Away

Seriously? In every game that I'm aware of, walking away signifies defeat or quitting. If I intend to bully someone, and they simply walk away, they have just told me that I was successful in "getting to them." Walking away only works if you make it clear that you are walking away without conceding defeat. I saw this strategy handled most elegantly by someone in eighth grade. Another student was baiting her. She looked the student up and down, shrugged, and said, "You're not worth my time." Then she walked away. *That* is how you walk away.

Stupid Advice #3: The Person Who Is Bullying You Has Low Self-Esteem (Part A) and He or She Might Change If You Are Nice to Him or Her (Part B)

Part A—The person bullying has low self-esteem. This assump-tion may be correct. It doesn't solve the problem. Additionally, some bullies thrive on power with no concurrent self-esteem deficits. In the above example, I mentioned that I "felt dirty" when I was writing it. That is because using power to hurt people is distasteful to me. I have heard physically strong men express contempt for men who hurt women. They are talking about the use of power to injure those who are vulnerable. By contrast, some people enjoy the power of hurting others. Hence, assuming that a bully is a good-hearted soul who is misguided and hoping to improve his or her self-esteem is naive and makes you vulnerable.

Part B—He or she might change if you are kind. Your tolerance and kindness will be perceived as weakness. Bullies understand strength, and they will perceive any soft approach as a weakness.

Optimal Strategy

Create distance from the bullies wherever and whenever you can. The focus is not about winning; it is about protecting yourself. In organizations, the degree to which you can buffer yourself from bullies depends on the hierarchy and what the culture tolerates. At one of my presentations on dealing with Difficult People, a young woman raised her hand.

"I am working with a bully," she said. "He makes negative comments about me and creates barriers when I try to do my job. Is there anything I can do?" I asked her about the hierarchy.

"The guys around him don't take it seriously," she responded. "They don't think it's a problem." I checked in on a few other questions, and the bottom-line answer was this: she needed to start looking for another job. It was a bummer because I wanted to help her figure out a way around it. The problem is that if you are in a subordinate position, and those in power are either bullying or tolerating the bullying, your options are limited. Even HR involvement has little success; we can't fire people for rolling their eyes at us or "accidentally" forgetting to give us critical information that we need to do our jobs.

I worked with a client who wanted to confront the bully directly and "let him have it." I continually dissuaded her because I did not want her to risk her reputation on his bad behavior. If you're going to confront a bully, you need to have an airtight strategy, organizational support, and a network of resources so that he is cornered with his hands tied. You walk into the confrontation, knowing that you are not alone and that you have already won. Most people I've met simply want to confront the bully and have no comprehensive strategy. This approach simply gives the bully information that he can further manipulate for his own agenda.

Let me explain my harsh stance on bullies and why it is so important to create distance. As I noted, bullies are good at "getting to us." The more exposure, the higher the likelihood that they will leave dents in our self-esteem. Perhaps you or someone you know was bullied in childhood or early adulthood. Bullying scars people such that they change their beliefs about themselves and others. These scars subconsciously or consciously guide later behavior in the areas of personal confidence, relationships, and risk-taking. Engaging with a bully, unless you know that you can win, exposes you to more poison. Even without direct confrontation, the cost of staying in the game is potentially high. If you remain close to a bully, simply to prove that he or she won't get to you, and then you spend the next five years recovering from the toxic work experience, who won?

Specific Strategies for When You Must Interact

1. Acknowledge to yourself that the bully can "get to you". For me, bullies and ice cream have something in common. Ice cream absolutely has the power to get to me. I have chosen not to keep it in the freezer. In acknowledging its power, I have the control.

2. Align yourself with power. If there is a person more powerful than the bully, align yourself with that person. Your alignment with someone powerful makes you less of a target because bullies respect power.

3. Feel power, show power. Forming your shield begins on the inside. We (psychologists, counselors, etc.) commonly recommend that children who are vulnerable to bullying engage in self-defense courses. It has nothing to do with being able to fight and everything to do with increasing confidence. When we are confident in ourselves, we walk differently. I will always say that bullies can smell fear. If you struggle with low self-confidence, work it out with a therapist.

    There are multiple ways to show power and confidence. Here are a few:
    - Maintain eye contact.
    - Call them out. "I know that you are trying to intimidate me. Are you bored?"
    - My favorite—that I have successfully used—"Try harder." (Instead of trying to ameliorate the conflict, you offer to escalate it. This statement shows power.)

- Don't give the bullies extra material. For example, "standing up" to a bully on email allows that person to twist your words and use them against you.
- Document. The person who documents has more power. Even if you feel silly writing down small events, a pattern of events will help anyone who is helping you. Whenever my clients have asked me if they are "reading into something," I rely on specific examples. The pattern of interactions helps me to draw an accurate conclusion.
- If you are in charge of a team and able to fire the bully, do so.
- Inform your social support system of what is going on. You need people around you who can help buffer you against the emotional damage of bullying.

MANIPULATIVE MARTIN

Description

Manipulative Martin may have several characteristics of the above personas. He may be manipulative and malicious, or he may have a pleasant game face such that it takes a while for people to see his true colors. Manipulative Martin may be so smooth and charming that his actions make you wonder if you are the crazy one. The term "gaslighting" refers to this phenomenon, whereby a person uses psychology and power strategies to make victims question their own sanity. Some Manipulative Martins are less dangerous—they simply want their way and use any means to get it.

Optimal Strategy

For a Manipulative Martin who seems harmless, stay consistent and firm. Consistency is vital for all Difficult People, but it is critical for Manipulative Martin. Otherwise, you will inadvertently reinforce the manipulation.

For the subtle and charming Manipulative Martins, you need to listen to your gut. Whether you believe it's the synthesis of subconscious cues, intuition, God, or a "spidey sense," listen to that little voice that makes you feel like something is wrong. Before you throw the book at me for giving you such vague advice, let me say this. I've known several very analytical people who claim to have no people skills and little ability to read other people. They *still* sense when something is "off." The key is to let go of logic and act based on your instinct.

Specific Strategies for When You Must Interact

1. For the harmless Manipulative Martin, you may want to let him know that you see his agenda. He will deny it, of course, but he will be more motivated to manipulate elsewhere.

2. For the charming, creepy Manipulative Martin, who makes you feel edgy and ill at ease, discuss the interactions with friends who can give you moral support. Cut the connection as soon as you can. If you have someone like this in your life, I can't tell you whether he is dangerous or not. Take your concerns seriously and get a support system.

3. If you are a subordinate to either of these Martins, don't engage the battle. If the organization can't see the problem, you may have to leave.

PENALTIES – HOLDING DIFFICULT PEOPLE ACCOUNTABLE IN THE WORKPLACE

For the Difficult People who create damage, you'll need to figure out penalties and tryout strategies. Early in this book, we discussed the principle that behavior speaks louder than words. Imagine that you are watching your favorite football game, and you notice targeting. Targeting occurs when a player uses forcible contact that goes beyond a legal tackle. It is considered one of the most egregious fouls. Suppose the referee walks over to the offender and says, "I want you to play nicely with the opposing team." Then the game continues as usual.

At the end of the season, commentators wonder why there is such a high incidence of targeting fouls. "I asked the referees about it. They said that they talked to the players and asked them not to do it. We just don't understand why it is still happening."

Talking is not a penalty. Talking is not a punishment. Talking only works when you are reprimanding a conscientious, responsibility-taking, emotionally mature performer. And that's not who we are talking about in this series, is it?

1. If someone needs to leave the game, document the infractions. Put them in a performance review if that is the process for your organization. Include HR. Make

sure that you have a 360 performance evaluation or
another system in place so that you can document
problems with bad attitudes and non-team-playing
behavior. If all of your measures focus on technical
skillsets, you will have a hard time justifying termination.
Be specific about the behavior and attitude problems and
the changes you need to see.

If you wait until you are at your wits' end to
document, you drag out the process. It's fair to give
someone the benefit of the doubt, but can't you do that
at the same time you are documenting? Otherwise, you'll
finally have your decision, but then you'll have to wait
several more months to complete the documentation
and transition process.

2. Praise people in group settings. Build a culture where
    the positive behavior gets openly praised—on email and
    in group settings. Even irrational people want to feel
    important and accepted. They will either adjust their
    behavior to garner praise or decide to play elsewhere.

3. *Do not ever* try to have heart-to-heart conversations with
    the Difficult Person. When people try to create insight,
    they make themselves and their teams vulnerable. If you
    are trying to figure out if they are coachable, give some
    behavior-based suggestions for improvement. Keep it
    specific and nonemotional.

4. Let your team know that you know what is going on and that you are working to resolve it. You may hesitate out of fear of being inappropriate, but your good team members need to feel that you have their back. You can keep it simple and professional without giving details.

Script: "I wanted to let you know that there are some problems in the interactions with X. I am working to resolve it. It may take a while. Could you please tell me if there are situations that occur, even if they feel trivial?"

5. Team members often don't want to be seen as tattletales or drama makers. Leaders who are hesitant to fire are often surprised by the number of validating stories that emerge after a Difficult Person leaves the department.

TRYOUTS – KEEPING DIFFICULT PEOPLE OUT OF YOUR ENVIRONMENT

1. Use the information discussed in chapter 7 on the protective power of other people, the pause, and due diligence. The extra effort will pay huge dividends.

2. Ask nonleading interview questions. If I am screening people on behalf of my clients, I ask questions that make it difficult for them to ascertain the inquiry's purpose.

Playing a different game with Difficult People will produce better results than the game you are currently playing. The change makes high achievers vulnerable to shifting back to their defaults because they believe that the problem has been resolved. In the next chapter, we will discuss the specific pitfalls you may encounter as you seek long-term success in dealing with Difficult People.

KEY TAKEAWAYS

1. *Develop a system to prevent Difficult People from entering your environment.*

2. *If you are already dealing with a Difficult Person, figure out which category (or categories) seems to match, and implement those strategies.*

3. *Document problems immediately, even when the infractions are subjective. The documentation pattern will provide a theme to support future actions, even if individual events appear innocuous.*

LEADERSHIP APPLICATION

I often tell people that the health or toxicity of an organization starts at the top and flows down. Our willingness to quarantine or fire Difficult People affects the health of the organization. Because Difficult People require energy, we can get caught up in the daily management of them. This myopic focus results in the number-one mistake of leading Difficult People: we grossly underestimate their damage to organizational morale and productivity. The second mistake occurs when we buy into the fear that they are irreplaceable. In fact, during editing, I learned that an organization promoted a Difficult Person to the C-suite to avoid losing her. This focus on skillset and indispensability causes us to miss the ripple effects that downgrade organizational success. If you are worried about replacing someone's skillset, think about how you would handle a sudden illness or voluntary departure, and use that information to generate a transition plan.

Chapter 13

CHANGING YOUR GAME

The first question that people ask me after they accept that someone is a Difficult Person is "Can this person change?" What they mean is "Will this person get better?" and "How long do I have to play a different game?" Just as you may be reticent to label someone as "difficult," you may loathe the energy requirement of changing your game. You can master interactions with Difficult People if you can

1. set appropriate expectations about someone's likelihood of changing;

2. figure out why you should put energy into changing your game; and

3. avoid the pitfalls that will derail your strategy.

CAN PEOPLE CHANGE?

In psychology, we try to answer questions about the development of personality. How much is genetic? How does the environment influence personality development? Does a person's personality change over time?

Here are the broad answers. Genetics plays a huge role. We know this from studies of identical twins who were raised in different environments but showed uncanny similarities in their life choices. We also know that people tend to have core personality traits that remain stable over time.

People can grow their strengths and mitigate their weaknesses, yet it is unlikely that a person's personality will dramatically shift. In terms of the Difficult People categories and some of the personality disorders they represent, significant change is rare. Most insurance companies do not cover the treatment of personality disorders because they perceive the problem as a long-term condition. Even though change can occur, it may take years. Core personality traits will usually change rapidly if brain trauma or other neurological events occur. Together, this means that positive change may not be in the amount or time frame necessary to alleviate a workplace or a relationship problem.

Accepting that people may not change can be painful. When we give up expectations of change, we save ourselves from the chaos, but then we grieve the loss of the relationship we always wanted. We also want to maintain hope and positive expectations for people, which leads us to mistake behavioral changes for personality changes.

Misattributions of Change

The following conversation is an example of a common scenario that plays out for my clients:

> *Bob:* "This is Sally's history. Here are the problems. She has been behaving this way with me for as long as I can remember."

> *Tricia:* "Okay, I know who this person is (i.e., personality type, motivations, triggers). Here is the strategy. I want you to say _____ and do _____ in every interaction."

Bob implements the strategy.

1 Month Later

> *Bob:* "Wow. This person is better. She has been more amicable. I'm hopeful here. I might need to relax my stance a bit and give her the benefit of the doubt."

> *Tricia:* "No, no. Please don't. Sally is behaving because we are playing a different game. Your responses (or lack thereof) are triggering the change. That does not mean she has changed on the inside. Stay the course."

One of two things happens at this point.

1. Bob listens to me and stays the course, so the situation improves.

2. Bob's internal need to be authentic wins; he drops his defenses and gets punched from behind as she reverts to her game. This setback not only upsets him emotionally; it substantially weakens his strategic position. When he dropped his defenses, he showed Sally more of his cards. We can recover the lost ground, but it will take longer.

Option B is the downside of believing the best in people without corresponding data. The people who do not want to be harsh or unforgiving get hurt at least three times before the logical argument wins over the emotional one. In relationships where the investment is high, the cycle of changing strategy, trusting too early, and getting hurt repeats itself many times. If this is you, please give grace and compassion to yourself. You are not stupid. You just want the relationship to work.

Assessing the Permanence of Change—the 2-Year Marker

If a person seems to change and has sustained that change for years, we have the data to hope that the difference may be permanent. The person approaches relationships in a qualitatively different fashion. At this point, we can start experimenting to see if the football game works. Suppose a person has a history of spreading personal information and creating drama. You haven't witnessed her doing this for 2 years. We can experiment by providing a tiny personal detail and seeing how she handles it. If she keeps the information confidential and seems to respect it, then you can gradually give more and continue to watch her response.

Why Start with 2 Years?

There is nothing magical about 2 years. You need a time frame that is long enough to account for normal variations in situations and internal motivations. I first learned to think in years when I researched and witnessed weight-loss patterns. Many people can sustain behavioral change for a finite amount of time. It is the reason why people often say that a diet "worked." For a limited amount of time, they followed the plan and experienced weight loss. Stress happens, life happens, schedules change—and the situational factors that supported weight loss 6 months ago may no longer be the same. Hence, many people can lose weight and keep it off for about a year, but the two-year mark seemed to allow a more accurate assessment of whether the new regimen can withstand internal and external pressures.

Similarly, an apparent personality change may be due to an increase in external rewards or the threat of loss. For example, one may be on his best behavior to obtain a promotion or rebuild a ruined relationship. The change can sustain itself for a while, but you need a time interval that is long enough for the immediate motivations to recede. When the initial incentives diminish (the promotion or relationship is no longer part of the picture) and external stressors enter the picture, we have the most accurate assessment of whether a permanent change has occurred. Essentially, you need to see a person's behavior when "life goes back to normal."

One Exception

I remember giving a presentation to a professional group about dealing with Difficult People. During the question-and-answer time, a woman raised her hand. She said, "I used to be one of the people you've described. I have a lot of those characteristics. I have been working hard to change it." I respected her vulnerability so much. She took personal responsibility, was nondefensive, and made no excuses.

It is rare, but if a person owns the problem, there is extra space for both grace and early optimism. They will struggle and often react in the "old" way, especially under stress. Yet they will be faster to recognize it, apologize, and shift to a healthier reaction. Even though they are a work in progress, this pattern is drastically different from what we see with most Difficult People. Most Difficult People do not take ownership; they blame everything and everyone else. If they accept responsibility, it is only for a short time and results from circumstantial pressure or temporary remorse. Then they shift back into the same pattern.

If a person is taking responsibility, seeking feedback, and working hard to change, you are witnessing someone who has an immense amount of courage. I would be more likely to support the person trying to change instead of quarantining them or using the other self-protective strategies in this book. Go slowly and be wise.

CAN YOU CHANGE? PUTTING DIFFICULT PEOPLE KNOWLEDGE INTO ACTION

If I had introduced Part IV with a long explanation about why it's essential to recognize and deal with Difficult People, you would have skimmed it. We all struggle with Difficult People, so we assume the knowledge is helpful. There is, however, a difference between the "knowing" and the "doing." Acting differently around toxic people takes courage. We often think that taking action might make things worse. We don't want to be mean. We worry about being wrong. To implement Difficult People strategies, you need to know "why" you want to change.

Using Your "Why" to Implement Changes

Here are the "whys" that help me to interact effectively with Difficult People, even when doing so makes me feel mean. *I feel called to make a difference in this world. I want to help as many people as possible, pursue excellence, show love to my friends and family, and keep myself healthy and happy.* All of these take a tremendous amount of energy, and I refuse to allow toxicity and the energy drain that goes with it into my life. I will be kind and compassionate, but I will not sacrifice the people and goals that I value on the altar of conflict avoidance.

What is your "why"? What purpose do you have that will get you from knowledge to action in the face of discomfort?

Chinks in Your Confidence Armor

If you have answers to your "why," the next step you need to take is assessing the chinks in your confidence armor. Are you worried that you will judge someone prematurely? Are you concerned that you might not apply the strategies correctly? (Let me help you with that—you're going to mess it up multiple times.)

I was in a leadership position years ago in which a subordinate was difficult. She had an attitude, could not be counted on, and underperformed. I thought about firing her, but I was worried that maybe it was "just me." When I finally took the opening to get her out, the other team members told me how uncomfortable they had been around her. They hadn't talked to me about it, because they knew that I was under stress. I had to admit that my lack of confidence had hurt others, and the shame of that forced me to act differently in the future.

Strategies to Increase Confidence with Difficult People

1. Make a list of areas where you struggle with confidence. If you can own and say "So what?" to your weaknesses, you have more power if Difficult People attempt to capitalize on them.

2. Acknowledge that Difficult People are masters of what they do. It's not about you.

3. Refuse to explain yourself and practice not explaining.

Pitfalls

Below is a list of the reasons people will read about Difficult People and not change course. If you are serious about quarantining Difficult People, watch out for these pitfalls.

Staying with Our Default Takes Less Energy

It takes a lot of energy to shift away from our default. If we listen to the red flags, we need to take action. With all of the competing commitments, we often feel like we do not have the emotional bandwidth to manage a situation. We default to hoping that it spontaneously gets better.

Commitment

Those of us who value commitment have a great deal of difficulty firing employees, firing clients, or distancing friends. We have already made an internal commitment to the person, so we feel responsible for maintaining the relationship. Usually, people with a high level of commitment take a high level of personal responsibility, so they try to fix the problem.

Sunk Costs

Sunk costs are those investments that we have already made, which we cannot recover. Below are statements from clients and friends that reveal an attempt to recapture sunk costs.

"We spent so much time hiring this person."
"I put 10 years into this friendship."
"We've already gone this far in building the business together."

It is easy to ignore the red flags if we are in relationships where we think that staying longer will somehow help us to "get our money back."

High Stakes

Below are some answers people have given me when I ask why they aren't willing to change their way of dealing with a Difficult Person.

"I am scared of a lawsuit."
"She will cut off the communication with my kids."
"There is a lot of money on the table."

It stands to reason that if the stakes are high, people may think that ignoring the red flags and hoping that everything will work is safer than rocking the boat. Use your trusted advisors to help you through high-stakes situations with Difficult People. They can identify blind spots and provide both the tactical and the emotional support that is difficult to acquire if you are on your own.

Difficult People always require a change in strategy. In the next chapter, you will learn about people who also benefit from a shift in approach but are not necessarily toxic.

KEY TAKEAWAYS

1. *Do not assume that a behavioral response to your tactical change reflects insight, character change, or personality improvement.*

2. *Do not assume that a behavioral response to your tactical change reflects insight, character change, or personality improvement.*

3. *Do not assume that a behavioral response to your tactical change reflects insight, character change, or personality improvement.*

Yes, I repeated that three times on purpose. Apart from trying to have rational conversations with irrational people, it is the single biggest mistake that high achievers make.

4. *You need a "why" to help you deal with Difficult People. Your answer will help you cope with the cognitive dissonance of playing a game that feels inauthentic.*

———————

Chapter 14

INTERACTING WITH PEOPLE WHO ARE INSECURE, HIGHLY ANXIOUS, OR SOCIAL-SKILL CHALLENGED

The socially inept person, the highly anxious person, and the insecure nontoxic person require different strategies, but they are unlikely to damage you. When you understand these individuals' characteristics, you can save energy and interact with them more effectively.

INSECURITY—TOXIC OR NOT?

There are two types of insecure people in the world. Most insecure people feel bad about themselves, but they don't take it out on others. Toxically insecure people make others pay for their insecurity. Not all people are toxically insecure, so how do you distinguish between the two groups?

Basic Insecurity

People who are basically insecure are unlikely to make their issues your issues. On a continuum, they may require more energy or compassion, but they have a level of kindness or self-awareness that allows them to be "good people." People who are personally insecure but not toxic will often be the first to acknowledge someone else's accomplishments. Even if they are negatively comparing themselves on the inside, they will be genuine cheerleaders.

Below are signs of basic insecurity. These individuals are fighting confidence battles, but they are unlikely to hurt you and may even be happy for your success.

Signs of Basic Insecurity

- They put themselves down.

- They verbally compare themselves to other people.

- They apologize for everything, even when it's not remotely linked to them.

- They walk with their head down, or their posture slumped.

- They physically make themselves small to not take up space, and they scurry out of the way for people whom they perceive as more powerful.

- They may dress in a way that makes them invisible.

- They are fearful of anything that might draw attention to themselves.

Managing Basically Insecure People

Basically insecure people are not a threat. You don't need to protect yourself as much as you need to be aware of your expectations and energy output. If you are a kind person, you may find yourself working extra hard to help an insecure person feel more confident. There is absolutely nothing wrong with doing this; you just need to understand that the path to increased confidence is a long and complex one. Sometimes you may believe in people more than they believe in themselves. Walk beside them and provide support, but understand that you cannot fight the battle for them.

Toxic Insecurity

Successful people threaten toxically insecure people. In the middle of writing about Difficult People, two people in my sphere were blindsided by toxically insecure people. One had a business partner who sold him out. The other had a new boss who terminated her, despite glowing reviews from subordinates and previous bosses. What did the two incidents have in common? The offenders were insecure and threatened.

Flags for Toxic Insecurity

1. Toxically Insecure People Will Twist Your Words. Toxically insecure people will make you pay by misinterpreting everything you say. They get defensive or offended easily, even when you have no hostile intentions. As a result, you will feel like you have to watch your words, and you will thus feel restricted from expressing your feelings or your opinions.

Note: A toxically insecure person in a romantic relationship or even a business partnership will twist your words and then ask you why you refuse to share your feelings. You'll distance yourself to self-protect, which will exacerbate their insecurity. If you notice this pattern, I strongly suggest reevaluating the viability of the relationship.

2. They Have Difficulty Praising Others. Toxically insecure people cannot get excited about someone else's success. Sometimes they will use the right words, but it feels fake, as if they are trying too hard. Toxically insecure people struggle with others' success because they think that someone else's spotlight is always at their own expense. The toxically insecure person may grudgingly acknowledge another person's success but then will add a negative comment to diminish it.

3. They "One-Up" Accomplishments. Everyone likes extra love sometimes, and some people are notorious braggarts. Toxically insecure people need their accomplishments to outshine others'. In the same way that they cannot share praise, they cannot share power. Hence, if someone else has an accomplishment, the toxically insecure people will always need to speak about their own triumphs.

Managing Toxically Insecure People

At the first meeting, when you see the first flag of insecurity, switch to being complimentary. If you are dealing with an insecure superior at work, you want to be slightly obsequious. I've used this strategy to decrease the chance that an insecure person will see me as a threat. In situations where I have needed to play the game, I have specifically made myself less powerful. I have stroked the toxically insecure person's ego by complimenting them and playing to their need for validation and control. If this makes you a bit nauseous, it should. There is a high price for continuous engagement with a toxically insecure person. The only way to manage him or her is to be less of yourself. You will want to hold your cards close, direct praise away from yourself, and accompany any possible rejection with additional ego-stroking.

If the toxically insecure person is a subordinate, focus on nurturing a team culture that rewards sharing praise and helping each other win. Sometimes a positive team dynamic will shut the toxically insecure person out. If the toxically insecure person is adversely affecting the team, you will need to intercede to protect morale.

HIGHLY ANXIOUS PEOPLE

You know you're dealing with highly anxious people when you spend a lot of time trying to reassure them that everything will be okay. They see threats around every corner. Their anxiety is sometimes palpable, making it difficult for the people around them to relax. Everyone worries sometimes. Some of us are naturally more anxious. On an anxiety scale of 1 to 10, this person seems to be consistently operating at 15.

First, understand that their reactions result from a combination of personality and brain chemistry. Situations might exacerbate it, but it is unlikely that you caused it or that you will be able to change it. Ultimately, the person will need to work with a mental health provider to bring their anxiety into the normal range.

Optimal Strategies

First, for those who of you who are really annoyed or frustrated by highly anxious people, check to see if you can figure out why their anxiety is difficult for you. If you had highly anxious parents, coping with anxious people can be triggering. Maybe you tend to take on others' emotions. This causes you to stress around anxious people. Understanding your reactions will not change the big picture, but it can help you with the patience and compassion to enact the following strategies.

Your primary strategy is to give reassurance and then change the topic or exit the conversation. Because a lot of anxiety relates to our thought processes versus real problems, problem-solving situations will only help temporarily. A lot of "what-ifs" govern the thought process of a highly anxious person. "What if this person doesn't like me?" "What if I make a mistake?" "What if my second, third, and fourth backup plans fail?" You can reassure one question, but as soon as you do, another one will pop up. The person isn't trying to be contrary or dismissive of your help. The brain is engaged in an unhelpful thought loop that continuously generates anxiety-producing scenarios.

The best way to be compassionate and save yourself from the emotional drain is to provide general reassurance. "Hang in there. It will be okay." Then, change the topic or exit the conversation.

This reassurance is *not* a good option for other relationships that you value. It is surface-level and unhelpful if someone is processing rationally and needs specific feedback to gain a different perspective. With the anxious person, diving into the detail to provide more meaningful reassurance will simply exhaust you.

If you are easily affected by other people's emotions, you need to limit your exposure to highly anxious people. If you need to interact regularly, use the protective techniques described in the emotional vomit section of chapter 5.

THE PERSON WHO DOES NOT READ SOCIAL CUES

Did you ever engage in a conversation where someone seemed deaf to your nonverbals? You back away, break eye contact, or limit responding, but they continue talking. When you say, "I have to go," they follow you to the door. Alternatively, they may say inappropriate things in public conversations with no awareness of the faux pas.

Some people have differences in neurological functioning that cause them to miss the nonverbal cues from others. All of us miss nuances sometimes. We may be distracted or preoccupied. People with neurological differences can be exceptional with informational processing but have difficulty reading social cues. They often come across as intelligent but odd.

Optimal Strategy

Use specific verbal statements instead of nonverbal cues. Vague comments do not work; the person will interpret their face value and miss the nuance.

Specific verbal statements:

"I can't talk to you anymore. I need to go."
"You are standing too close to me. Please back up."

You will feel rude. The clear, focused statements help not only you but also the other person. People who can't read social cues often know that something is wrong, but they don't know what they should do differently. It's as if everyone else is speaking a secret language that they don't understand. I have often deconstructed social skills into precise phrases, gestures, and cues to help clients who lacked the innate comprehension of these nonverbals. I have said to them, "You can't say that; it makes you look weird. Say this instead." Nobody gets offended. Rather, they are happy to have the exact recipe for what they need to do. If you can force yourself to spell out what they can do differently, you help them and yourself.

One of my friends was frustrated with a nonsocial team member. As a leader, my friend values team collaboration.

"Tricia," he said, "I just want this team member to be more social with everyone else."

"What did you say to him?" I asked.

"Well, exactly that. I told him that it would be good for him to be more social and interactive with his colleagues."

My reply: "No, no, no. That's not specific enough. He won't understand it. You need to say, 'John, when you come in each morning, I want you to pass by each desk and say hello within the first 20 minutes of arriving.'" This specific, non-nuanced instruction removes ambiguity and allows people without innate social skills to succeed.

KEY TAKEAWAYS

1. *People who are insecure, highly anxious, or socially challenged need a professional to help them change. Unless you are a therapist, be careful about the investment you make in trying to help them.*

2. *If you do not see red flags, you can give extra kindness or specific feedback without worrying that they will use the information against you.*

3. *Direct and specific feedback is helpful to socially challenged people. They are unlikely to get offended because they find the clarity refreshing.*

LEADERSHIP APPLICATION

You can help your team by giving them the tools for interacting with an insecure, anxious, or socially inept team member. Even if there is no toxicity involved, team members may feel stressed because they don't know how to handle the interactions. You can have workshops on navigating personality styles, broach the subject when someone brings it up, or provide some strategies during one-on-ones. Hold the conversations in a respectful tone that honors people's differences. Acknowledge the challenges, and everyone will win.

In Parts I through IV, we discussed the idiosyncrasies of humans and how to address them. You noticed multiple scripts in which I suggested phrases that you could use in specific situations. Part V focuses specifically on scripts, answering the question "But how do I say that?"

HOW DO I SAY THAT?

Chapter 15

SCRIPT FUNDAMENTALS

While teaching my clients how to understand themselves and others, I heard one question over and over: "How do I say that?" The question behind the question is "How do I say that without being offensive or making the problem worse?" People often are either afraid to speak up or they speak with no awareness of context. Both of these behaviors reduce your effectiveness. If you do not use your voice, you are powerless. If you comment without awareness of context or others' feelings, you look like a jerk. The middle ground is a nuanced approach that accounts for your own needs and the needs of others.

Knowing what to say in awkward situations can increase trust in positive relationships and set boundaries in negative ones. If you find yourself questioning your right to impose a limit or make a request, work on these personal areas of insecurity as you build your script competence.

In this chapter, you will learn script fundamentals and specific tips that will help you across all situations. We will start with three concepts to keep in mind when you are trying to figure out what to say: know what you want to achieve, think in terms of win-win, and account for the presence of emotion.

KNOW WHAT YOU WANT TO ACHIEVE

Figure out what you want to achieve when you are choosing what to say. If your only intention is to let someone know how you feel, you may exacerbate the problem. Once we define the goal, context, and people involved, we can make wise decisions about what to say and what not to say.

Here are some of the outcomes that people want:

"I want to express what I need without hurting his or her feelings."
"I need to give critical feedback without ruining the relationship."
"I need to express a problem without making myself look weak."
"I need to set a boundary."
"I need this person to take me seriously. (This means: "I want them to change their behavior.")

THINK WIN-WIN VERSUS RIGHT-WRONG

I was in the gym the other day, watching one of those "What house will we buy?" shows. The spouses were at odds about staying in their current home or moving to a new one. After a heated disagreement, one spouse said, "Look, I know how difficult moving feels because your dad built our house. This is going to have to be your decision." Instantly, the other person softened his stance. "I know there are limitations with our current home," he said.

And there it is, I thought. *If someone acknowledges another person's viewpoint, even a little, people can move from impasse to compromise.* No one likes to be made wrong. Everyone wants to feel heard, even if the other person disagrees. When we are trying to prove that we are right, we automatically put the other person in the "wrong" position. On the other hand, saying "I see your perspective" lowers the boxing gloves and allows a conversation to begin.

The implementation of a win-win strategy starts inside of you. If your goal is to prove that you are right and the other person is wrong, your intention will show, no matter what words you use.

ACCOUNT FOR THE PRESENCE OF EMOTION

Have you ever had an argument with your partner where you felt like you couldn't "get through," and after an hour, the two of you couldn't remember why you were arguing? People hear our emotions rather than our words.

Emotion shades much of our communication. Your focus on the feelings of both you and your conversational partner will always be more important than the specific words. Ignoring emotion is fatal.

Tips for Managing Emotions in Communication

1. **Take a break.** If you have a disagreement about one topic and shift to another issue, the second topic will feel like an argument because of the emotional carryover. Take a break or use humor to break the emotional intensity and refocus.

2. **In times of high emotion, wait for emotions to recede.** If you need to respond in the moment, say, "I have a strong reaction to this at the moment; I'd like some time to think about it."

3. **Wait until you are rested and alert.** Fatigue, coupled with high emotion, distorts the mental clarity that we need for optimal scripts.

4. **"Call out" the emotion.** Don't assume that you can mask it. Other people feel it, even if they don't understand where it is coming from. Humans are fantastic at creating negative scenarios to fill in knowledge gaps. When they feel your emotion, whatever scenario they imagine will be worse than the actual one. Give simple explanations—that a conversation is hard for you, that you can't find the right words, or that you might hurt someone's feelings. This strategy allows the person to focus on the truth of the exchange rather than the conjecture that may arise from unexplained undercurrents.

   When people know your intentions, they will help you through the words. One of the heartwarming patterns

that I have noticed about my clients is that they help
me say difficult things. I push my clients hard, but I am
simultaneously protective of them. So when I pause and
say, "I'm worried about how to say this," they often say,
"It's okay; go ahead." They try to help me say the words
that might hurt them. You see, when people understand
our intentions, the outcome works. Our terms might
be mangled, our concepts unclear, and our metaphors
atrocious—but those flaws matter only to us. When we
pull back the curtain just a little to let someone understand
the emotional backstory of our intentions, magic happens.
We turn the discussion from a tense one into an exchange
between humans who are trying to muddle through life
and help each other.

5. **Give someone a heads-up when you might hurt their
   feelings.** In relationships with people who want me to be
   super-straightforward, I say, "Brace yourself. This is going
   to hurt." The brief comment gives the other person the split
   second to understand that emotional impact is coming.
   That nanosecond provides a buffer and keeps him or her
   from being blindsided. For people who prefer a softer touch,
   I say, "I need to say something that might hurt, and that's
   not my plan. You know I think you're fabulous." Then I go
   right into it. After you give the tiny heads-up, *do not* drag
   out the pause and add a lot of additional words. Nobody
   likes to wait for 45 minutes (or 15 minutes) to hear the
   bad things you might say. The waiting creates anticipatory

anxiety, which is one of the most difficult human emotions. As the tension increases, your chances of having a quality conversation and optimal outcome decreases.

SOMETIMES YOU WILL FEEL STUPID

It is impossible to "get it right" all the time. Even with the knowledge that I am transmitting to you, I have had epic failures. I have hurt people's feelings, tried too hard to avoid hurting their feelings, and made incorrect assumptions. It's humbling since I'm supposed to be the expert on getting it right. Emotions and humans are messy, and learning what to say and how to say it requires patience with others and with ourselves.

TIPS FOR SAYING THINGS WITHOUT ALIENATING PEOPLE

- **Reject the idea, not the person.**
  "I know you've put a lot of effort into this. The part that I disagree with is..."

- **Use "we" or "i" to decrease conflict.** Using the word "you" instantly creates conflict (me versus you). It can come across as accusatory or presumptuous. Use "we" or "I" whenever possible.

- **What comes after the "but" matters the most.** Put the tough stuff before the "but," and words of affirmation after. Read these two sentences.

"I'm upset that you forgot about our appointment, but I still like you."

"I still like you, but I'm upset that you forgot our appointment."

- **Tone of voice trumps words.** Pay attention to your tone, and err on the side of making your voice softer and slower.

Difficult People Warning: Difficult People will accuse you of yelling or being defensive to make you feel guilty for using your voice.

- **Figure out what you can truthfully say to avoid feeling fake.** If you are worried about feeling fake or coming across as inauthentic, figure out what you can truthfully say. Use this thought: *What can I say that is nicer than what I want to say but still has a kernel of truth such that I can keep my integrity intact?*

- **Look for common ground.**
  "I know this matter stresses you out also."
  "I know that we both want this business to win."

In this chapter, we discussed the relational elements that facilitate optimal interactions. In the next chapter, you will learn the specific components of scripts. We will then cover sample situations so that you can understand script infrastructure and build your own.

KEY TAKEAWAYS

1. *Focus on what you want to achieve and how you want people to feel when the conversation is over.*

2. *You can say almost anything when the other person feels that you are valuing him or her.*

Chapter 16

SCRIPTS

D o you remember middle school English, when you had to learn how to diagram the components of a sentence? Scripts work that way, only they are more fun. If we reverse-engineer scripts that work, we can see recurring components that operate among many scripts. These recurring components help us to express needs, set boundaries, and give feedback.

Below, you will find a list of script components. Read through them, and then pay attention to how they are used in the situational scripts that follow. These components will help you formulate appropriate scripts for all situations.

SCRIPT COMPONENTS

- **Colloquial** (casual, informal speech): Used to decrease emotional intensity

- **Clarification:** Used to make sure that you heard the other person correctly; also used occasionally to let the other person hear the absurdity of a statement

- **Feeling:** Hurt, excited, frustrated, stressed. Used to express your feeling or to let people know that you heard theirs.

- **Feeling with downgrade:** Bothered, concerned, confused. Used to decrease intensity. Downgrade vulnerable emotions to increase the other person's emotional safety. For example, if you think someone is scared, downgrade it to "upsetting." This strategy protects them from having to admit to vulnerable emotion (generally fear or hurt). You can also downgrade your own feelings for your own comfort or when you need to make a check-in feel casual.

- **"No" statement:** Sets a boundary

- **Affirmation:** Shows value to the other person or his or her idea

- **Statement of position:** Clear statement of "where you're at"

- **Noncommittal show of position:** Vague statement that indicates you disagree. Used where you feel that you need to "take a stand" but do not want to escalate conflict

- **Use of opponent's momentum:** Agreement. Used to respond to someone attacking you.

- **Acknowledgment of potentially being wrong:** Used to apologize; also used to indicate that you don't "have to be right." This acknowledgment lowers defensiveness and opens the door to resolving conflict.

- **Social apology:** Used for a conciliatory approach. This is not an acknowledgment of doing something wrong; rather, it may lessen another person's emotional reaction.

- **Need statement:** Stating what you want or need

- **Sequenced repetition:** Making exactly the same statement, with the words in the same sequence, multiple times. This fundamental is most commonly used in scripts when someone is trying to push against your boundaries.

- **Removal of pressure statement:** Plays to the need for autonomy and reduces psychological reactance

- **Heads-up:** Allows person to brace himself for hurt. It also can be used to create expectations of the worst, such that the actual information is seen as more positive.

- **Pause creation:** Allows you to create the space to avoid giving an opinion or answer in the moment

- **Distraction:** Used to redirect the person's attention away from an inflammatory topic

- **No-yes:** Shows value of the other person while setting boundaries. Softens rejection. "I can't come to the party, but I would love to see the pictures afterward."

- **Asking for help:** Asking for help engages the other person's altruism, sends the sense of being "in it together," and decreases any potential perception of criticism.

Situational Scripts

Scripts, like all effective communication, are hard. We are trying to transmit facts, emotions, and intentions across space and into another person's brain with the hope that he or she will be able to understand them exactly as we feel and see it in our own mind. If your words come out the wrong way, just own it. If you don't know if you make sense, ask the other person what he or she heard you saying. If you see scripts in this section that resonate, practice saying them out loud until they come fluently off your tongue.

This last section is formatted for quick reference. You will be able to find all of the script headings in the table of contents. You can find your current situation or scripts of interest by browsing through the headings. Familiarize yourself with the scripts present, and then refer back to them as you need. I've included the rationale and component breakdown for each script, as well as some prevention tips, leadership applications, and follow-up action steps.

UNIVERSAL APPLICATION

How to Apologize

Situation	You've messed up. Even if the whole situation is not your fault, you still contributed.
Script	*I want to take responsibility and apologize for _____. I am going to do _____ in the future to prevent it from happening again.*

Component	Phrase
Acknowledgment of wrong	*I want to take responsibility and apologize...*

Rationale	Taking responsibility adds to your integrity. A straight-up apology with actions to match shows the other person that you care.
Leadership Application	If you want a team who takes ownership for their actions, you must lead by example.

How to Give Compliments

Situation	An employee does a good job on a project.
Script	*I noticed that you put a lot of effort into making sure the details were accurate. Thank you.*

Component	Phrase
Affirmation	*I noticed that you put a lot of effort...*

Rationale	Giving a specific compliment is more meaningful than a general one. It helps team members to know that you notice their specific efforts. Extensive compliments can make people feel embarrassed. Keep it short and specific.
Leadership Application	Draw attention to what you want to increase. You can use compliments to make people feel valued, to increase their level of performance, or to build a culture around what is noticed and rewarded.

Someone Won't Take No for an Answer

Situation	Someone wants you to do something that you do not want to do and will not take no for an answer.
Script	*I'm sorry; I can't accommodate you. (They persist.) I'm sorry; I can't accommodate you. (They persist.) I'm sorry; I can't accommodate you.*

Component	Phrase
Social apology	*I'm sorry.*
"No" statement	*I can't accommodate you.*
Sequenced repetition	*"I can't accommodate you"* is repeated exactly the same each time.

Rationale	If someone doesn't take your first no as an answer, say the exact same phrase in sequence, each time they persist. Do not change wording. Do not change tone. Many people try to explain or say no in a different way. The other person's brain perceives these deviations as a signal that he or she may be able to convince you. When you use the exact same phrase redundantly, it metaphorically allows the other person to run into a brick wall, and he or she will give up.
Leadership Application	This strategy will help you deal with difficult subordinates.

Someone Hurts Your Feelings

Situation	Your friend/partner/colleague said something that tweaked you the wrong way. The relationship is worth keeping.
Script	*I want to check in with you for a second on something. The other day when we were speaking about X, I thought you said _____. I know it's not a big deal, but it's been bothering me.*

Component	Phrase
Colloquial	*I want to check in with you for a second on something.*
Clarification request	*I thought you said _____.*
Your feeling with downgrade	*It's been bothering me.*

Rationale	If someone doesn't take your first no as an answer, say the exact same phrase in sequence, each time they persist. Do not change wording. Do not change tone. Many people try to explain or say no in a different way. The other person's brain perceives these deviations as a signal that he or she may be able to convince you. When you use the exact same phrase redundantly, it metaphorically allows the other person to run into a brick wall, and he or she will give up.
Leadership Application	This strategy will help you deal with difficult subordinates.
Alternative Script for Leaders	*I heard you say ___ yesterday, and I was confused. Can you help me understand?*

Rationale	You can call attention to the statement in a noncommittal way, such that you do not risk power loss. The word "confused" doesn't put people on the spot, yet the phrase "Can you help me understand?" holds them accountable.
Contraindication	**Difficult People Warning:** *Do not, under any circumstance,* use this with an irrational or toxic person. Showing vulnerability only works with people who are level-headed and compassionate.
Follow-Up Action	There usually isn't one. However, if the person says/ does the same thing again, it means that there is a deeper issue. You can start by saying, "Can you help me understand why this is happening?"

You Need to Give Information That
Someone Doesn't Want to Hear

Situation	Someone has information that is incorrect, and he or she is going to act accordingly.
Script	*You're (probably) going to hate this. Sigh. Here's the (thought/information/research). I know it's your decision, though.*

Component	Phrase
Heads-up	*You're (probably) going to hate this.*
Removal of pressure	*It's your decision, though.*

Rationale	"You're going to hate this" lets the other person know that you understand him, calls out the obvious, and makes him more receptive. Add "probably" because people dislike being told what they are thinking/feeling. Some people will be more receptive, just to prove you wrong. "It's your decision, though" recognizes their autonomy and removes reactance.

Someone Says Something That Doesn't Make Sense

Situation	Someone says something that makes no sense, but you don't want to make them "wrong."
Script	*Let me make sure I understand you correctly. What I heard you saying is _____. Did I get it right?*

Component	Phrase
Clarification	*What I heard you saying is _____. Did I get it right?*
Rationale	1. Some people will instantly hear the problem as soon as they hear their thoughts repeated. 2. Even if they don't see a problem, your response pattern indicates that you think there is one. 3. Having them repeat what they said gives you a few seconds to collect yourself and figure out your next step.

You Want to Ask for a Favor without Creating Pressure

Situation	You have a proposal that you would like your colleague to review, but you know that he or she is already pressed for time.
Script	*I would love your set of eyes on this proposal, but I also know that you have a lot on your plate. Is there a time that would be optimal for you to check out a few paragraphs? If not, I can figure out other options.*

Component	Phrase
Affirmation (implied)	*I would love to get your eyes. (The request itself shows that you value the other person's input.)*
Acknowledgment of their feeling, downgraded	*I also know that you have a lot on your plate. (You are alluding to stress without assuming that they are stressed.)*
Removal of pressure	*If not, I can use other options. (Only use this if you have other options.)*
Rationale	First, you are acknowledging that you are adding stress. Second, you are making it clear that you know life will go on if they say no. Many people will squeeze it in because you asked so nicely, but they'll appreciate the option to say no and know that it won't hurt the relationship.
Contraindication	*Never* say, "No pressure, no rush, or take your time," if this is not true. These statements, intended to remove pressure, signal to the other person's brain that it's low priority.

You Disagree with the Recommendation
of Someone You Respect

Situation	Your friend is a professional who has given you input on a situation. You respect her expertise, but you've also read a lot of counterapproaches that resonate better with you.
Script	*Thank you so much for the information. I need to think about this a little more and look at the different angles. I may ask for a follow-up conversation on this.*

Component	Phrase
Affirmation	*Thank you, I may ask for a follow-up conversation.*
Pause creation	*I need to think about this a little more...*

Rationale	The "thank you" and the comment that you may follow up shows that you recognize her intention and her expertise. The comment about thinking a little more sends the message that you are going to incorporate her information and other information to figure out what might be best.

You Need to Ask a Question of a
Long-Winded Conversationalist

Situation	You need to speak with someone who talks forever.
Script	*Just a heads-up before we dig in, I have a (meeting / dinner / other call) in 15 minutes. I don't want you to feel cut off if we need to wrap abruptly.*

Component	Phrase
Heads-up	*Just a heads-up*
Feelings statement, downgraded	*I don't want you to feel cut off. (You are alluding to the possibility of hurt feelings without calling it out.)*
Need statement	*If we need to wrap abruptly*
Rationale	You know this person will likely keep talking, even when you say that you need to go. If you apprise him of the time limitation on the front end, you will feel more comfortable disengaging.
Prevention	Use email or text whenever possible. If you must engage in an in-person or phone conversation, schedule them in low-productivity time when your brain is half-dead anyway. Wherever possible, back them against meetings or other calls so that you have a nonnegotiable exit to the conversation.

You Ask for Information to Plan,
and You Don't Receive a Response

Situation	You need to know someone's availability to coordinate a meeting or social event. You ask which day would be best to meet. You don't receive an answer.
Script	*I have this thing about planning. It's hard for me when I don't have firm dates and times. Could we plan for ___, and can you let me know as soon as possible if something comes up?*

Component	Phrase
Statement of position	*I have this thing about planning.*
Your feeling, downgraded	*It's hard for me.*
Request for help	*Could we plan for ___, and can you let me know as soon as possible if something comes up?*
Rationale	Planners assume that spontaneous people are flaky. Spontaneous people assume that planners are rigid. If you make the conversation about which style is right, it comes across as a personal accusation. Shift the focus to asking a person for help. Most people are happy to comply. Alternately, some people are overwhelmed by the decision-making process of planning. When you provide specific options, you help them, and you avoid the frustration build that occurs from waiting for him or her to make a decision.

Tricia Notes on "I have this thing about planning..."	This phraseology is very colloquial, but it lets people know I have emotion connected to the preference. Before I used this phrase, I stated a basic preference, such as "Please let me know if your schedule changes." Once I added that hint of emotion, that it is a personal "thing," I saw immediate positive changes in terms of people providing information on scheduling.
Follow-Up Actions	If the person does not respond and later wants you to make last-minute adjustments to your plan, you'll need to say no. "I'm sorry; I'm not able to do that" *or* "I'd love to help you, but I already made plans." These responses set the precedent that your style doesn't accommodate last-minute planning.

Someone Is Lying to You and You Know It

Situation	You catch someone contradicting himself or herself. It's obviously more than a slip of tongue.
Script	*I'm confused. Maybe I misunderstood. I thought you said...*

Component	Phrase
Your feeling, downgraded	*I'm confused.*
Clarification	*I thought you said...*

Rationale	1. There is no script that will fix bad character. 2. You want to acknowledge the lie so that he or she knows that you aren't stupid. Otherwise, the assumption will be that you are naive / didn't catch it. 3. Using "I'm confused; I misunderstood" (clarification request) is nonconfrontational, *and* in their attempt to talk themselves out of it, they will give you even more information. 4. The reason you want them to give you more information / dig themselves into a deeper hole is that this information helps you to know the extent to which you need to quarantine or eliminate their influence.

HIGH-STAKES NEGOTIATION

You Need to Draw a Bottom Line in a Negotiation

Situation	You are negotiating a high-stakes deal or settlement. You have conceded multiple points, but the other party is not making similar concessions. Rather, he continues to push you to let go of additional equity, money, or other assets.
Script	**Script 1:** *I can't do that.* Additional justification, explanation, and emotional manipulation from other party. **Script 2:** *I can't do that.* Other party continues to add pressure. **Script 3:** *I can't do that.* *Important:* Keep nonverbals consistent. Use the same even tone inflection and flat facial expression each time.

Component	Phrase
Sequenced repetition	*I can't do that.*

Rationale	First, as mentioned a few other times in this book, using the exact same phrase three times in a row is attention-grabbing. In this case, it also lets the opposition know that they have hit a wall. The combination of using exactly the same words and showing no tone/facial variation gives them nothing to do. Suddenly, you are holding the cards because you've sent the message that any tactic they try will be useless. Be warned, though, that if you change your wording or expression at all, you will send a message that they might have an opening, and the process will take longer.

You Need to Figure Out How to Calm Down
a Boss, Investor, or Business Partner

Situation	The stakes are high and the other person is freaking out.
Script	*I know that we've reviewed ___, ___, and ___ problems. Talk to me about the additional concerns you have, so I can help.*

Component	Phrase
Clarification	*I know that we've reviewed ___, ___, and ___ problems.*
Acknowledgment of other person's feelings, downgraded	*Talk to me about the additional concerns.*
Rationale	In high-stakes situations, people's anxiety increases. The increased anxiety often spills out onto those around them in the form of frustration or anger. It's common to become defensive or respond to the specific variables at hand. What you want to do is to address the underlying emotion. First, when you rephrase what you already know about the other person's concerns, you show that you've been listening. When a person feels heard, his anxiety lessens. Next, "Talk to me about your additional concerns" helps them to get at some emotional variables that may be driving their reactions. Offering to help shows that you are committing to solving the problem. It also gives the other person emotional support without putting him or her on the defensive by calling out stress, anxiety, etc. (Some people will not want to admit the emotional vulnerability.) Even if anxiety is not driving the other person's emotional upset, this script will get them to talk more and give you information about what is going on.

WORK

Someone Asks You to Engage in a Dual-Role Situation

(Dual role—a client wants to meet with you socially; a friend wants you to do business; a family member wants you to hire him or her)

Situation	You are hiring an employee and one of your clients suggests his or her daughter. You're concerned that it may jeopardize the relationship if things don't work out.
Script	*Your daughter sounds impressive. I've had some tough experiences with hiring family members, so I've just made it a policy not to do so. Having said that, I would be happy to speak with your daughter and learn her skillset so that I can keep my eyes open for her.*

Component	Phrase
Position statement	*I've just made it a policy not to do so.*
Affirmation	*I would be happy to speak with your daughter and learn her skillset.*

Rationale	You want the soft let-down to maintain the relationship. When you turn down a dual-role request, the trick is to make sure that people know it's not personal. If you can refer to a license, a personal policy, or a concern about making sure that you don't inadvertently hurt someone, it helps the listener understand that your stance is about the big picture rather than him or her. Adding an offer to help in a different way further shows that the rejection is not personal. In some cases, you can be up-front and say, "I value this relationship and I don't want to jeopardize it in any way if things go sideways."

Prenup	If you decide to engage in dual-role situations, please discuss a prenup. A prenup is a discussion of what you will do if the dual-role relationship gets messy. How will we separate if this setup doesn't work? How can we preserve the existing friendship / family relationship if we need to part ways on the business side?

A Subordinate Will Not Take No for an Answer

Situation	One of your direct reports continues to ask for a raise for herself and the team. You have explained the logistical constraints multiple times.
Script	*I can't do that. As we've discussed before, the organization has a pause on promotions. I will let you know if or when that changes.*

Component	Phrase
"No" statement	*I can't do that.*

Rationale	Specifically say no and why you are saying no. Sometimes people ask repeatedly because we have softened our "no" and left the window of hope open. The addition of "I will let you know if or when that changes" shows that you expect he or she will not persist.
Leadership Application	Rational people take "no" as an answer the first time. When someone persists and pushes against your authority, it may signal a Difficult Person. Staying firm shuts down the situation faster and diminishes oxygen to the entitled, martyrs, and drama-oriented folks.

You Are a Professional and Someone
Wants Advice on the Weekend

Situation	You are a medical doctor, attorney, psychologist, tax advisor...and someone wants to dump a scenario on you when you are in the middle of your much-needed playtime.
Script	*I'm happy to talk with you, but I'll be honest, my brain isn't focused right now. I want to make sure that I can give you my full attention and the best information. Could you call my office on Tuesday?*

Component	Phrase
Pause creation	*My brain isn't focused right now.*
Affirmation	*I'm happy to talk with you.*
No-yes	*Could you call my office on Tuesday?*

Rationale	You want to let them know that you want to be helpful but that you aren't available right now. If you might see this person again, you want to set a precedent that you don't talk shop on weekends. By commenting that you want to provide full attention, you affirm their importance. By offering to speak with them on a follow-up day, you are figuring out how to say yes in the middle of saying no, thus minimizing rejection.
Preventive	Don't open the door. Especially if you are a "helper," you will want to share just a little bit of information. That 15 minutes will morph into 45 minutes before you know it. You don't have to talk about your professional life. You don't have to offer advice. It's okay to sit and keep that fabulous knowledge inside of you for two days.

Someone Asks If You Have a Minute—You Don't

Situation	You are in the middle of something, and someone asks if you have a minute.
Script	*Is this urgent or can I catch up with you at 2 p.m.? I want to give you my full attention, and I'm worried that I would be distracted if we talk right now.*

Component	Phrase
Clarification	*Is this urgent?*
No-yes	*Can I catch up with you at 2 p.m.?*
Affirmation	*I want to give you my full attention.*
Your feeling	*I'm worried.*

Rationale	The clarification lets people know that you are willing to interrupt your work for urgent matters, but not for something that can wait. If the person says it's urgent, and it's not, you'll know for future reference. The specific alternate suggestion makes people feel important and secure. It shows that you are not just brushing them off and lets them know that they will get the answers they want. Commenting on your feelings (worry, distraction) helps them want to help you.
Additional Benefit	People often problem-solve or manage their emotions when you are not immediately available. Thus, the conversation is likely to be more productive, and sometimes they won't need you after all.

Preemptive	Teach people how you operate. When people first meet me, I often say, "I run on two different levels. I'm not open to small talk when I'm focused and working hard. I want you to know, though, that if something bad is happening, it's personally important for me to be available." I get few interruptions, but people feel safe asking if something serious is happening.

Someone Is a Long-Winded Conversationalist

The Wall of Talk

© Dr. Tricia Groff

Situation	You are at work. You want to get work accomplished. A colleague wants to engage in a long story. You either like the person or are worried about hurt feelings if you do an abrupt cutoff.
Script	*I'm sorry. I need to interrupt for a second. I'm a little distracted because I'm in a time crunch for this project. I would love to hear the rest of the story. Can I catch up with you at 3 p.m.?*

Component	Phrase
Social apology	*I'm sorry.*

Need statement	*I need to interrupt for a second. I'm in a time crunch for this project.*
Affirmation	*I would love to hear the rest of the story.*
Rationale	Cutting off a talker can make both you and the talker feel like there is some type of rejection happening. There is. You are rejecting ongoing use of time for their thoughts. The only way to soften it is with a social nicety like an apology or affirmation and the reason you wish to end the conversation.
Follow-Up Actions	If the person continues to talk, get up and leave the space. If it is in your space, offer to walk him or her to wherever they are going next. If it is in shared space, go to the bathroom, get a drink, etc. "You know what, I need to get a drink before digging back into work. Do you want to walk me there?"
Nonverbals Tips to Shorten Conversations	Do not ask questions. Do not smile. Do not nod. Do not show any engagement.
End of the Road	If you have already told them that you need to go back to work and they are not responding, all of the end-of-the-road options will feel rude. You may simply have to hang up the phone or turn your back to them until they go away. You are not responsible for managing someone else's social deficit.

In physical settings, close the door, change the seating arrangement, or use headphones. In virtual settings, use "do not disturb." People's brains go like this. "See Mike. Talk to Mike." How does this interface with open-door policies, 24/7 availability, and instant customer service? It doesn't. My goal in this book is to protect your sanity and increase your excellence. There is no sanity or excellence without boundaries.

Do not initiate a conversation if you are working. You may think that it will be a 5-minute conversation, but when you open the door or say "How are you?" you lose control of time.

Prevention

If you must engage, say, "I only have 7 minutes, but I wanted to answer your question." This allows you to more easily shut down the conversation. Additionally, the use of "7" is attention-grabbing. It's not the colloquial 5, 10, or 15 minutes, and so it shows the person that you are tracking time tightly.

Cutting off people you genuinely like and want to have a relationship with is hard for both of you. Tell people ahead of time what to expect, so that they don't start the story in the first place. For example, let your colleagues know that you are super-focused in the morning but will try hard to be available at lunch in order to stay up-to-date with work and social updates.

Do not send mixed messages. If you want to train people not to interrupt you within a certain time frame, you can't initiate or maintain conversation simply because you are bored or procrastinating in a given moment.

Someone Is Holding You Hostage at a Business-Social Event

Situation	You are at a networking event, and you suddenly find yourself held hostage in a conversation. The person is not reading your nonverbals or subtle attempts to move on.
Script	*I hate to interrupt you; I need to (go to the bathroom/catch this colleague/go get water). It was great talking to you.* or *It was nice speaking with you. There is a person across the room I would like to meet. I hope you have a good evening.*

Component	Phrase
Social apology	*I hate to interrupt you.*
Need statement	*I need to (go to the bathroom/catch this colleague/go get water).*
Affirmation	*It was great talking to you.*
Action	Interrupt, make the statement, and smile as you walk away.
Rationale	If you wait for the other person to acquiesce and release you, you will be standing there for another 15 minutes.
Preventive (External)	One of my friends sets alarms to go off at certain intervals or 15 minutes before he leaves. This external stimulus provides the interruption and allows him to say that it is his reminder to make a call, get to a meeting, etc.
Preventive (Internal)	Know what you want out of social events, and have a bit of a game plan ahead of time. Remember that your needs matter too.

You Need to Give Negative Feedback to a Subordinate

Preemptive	If you are in a position to give feedback, it is helpful to find out right at the beginning how people prefer to receive it. Most people fall into two categories—those who like a sandwich to soften (positive, negative, positive) and those who want to hear it straight.
Script	**First Incident:** *I noticed _____. Can you help me to understand your thought process / what you were trying to achieve / what went wrong?* **Second Incident:** *I noticed ___ again, and I thought we had arrived at ____ solution. What needs to happen differently for you to succeed?* **Third Incident:** *We've had several discussions about _____. I need to put you on a formal improvement plan. This is what I need to see by these dates. Here are the consequences if I do not see them. (Honestly, if conversations 1 and 2 were clear, you may be bidding this person good-bye. Good employees will have already fixed the problem or enlisted you for help in how to do so.)*

Component	Phrase
Observation	*I noticed _____.*
Open-ended question	*Can you help me to understand your thought process?* *What needs to happen differently for you to succeed?*
Rationale	A specific observation helps everyone win. It helps the motivated employee know how to succeed; it provides documentation to fire the unmotivated one.
Speaking to Strength	For someone who needs a softer touch, speak her potential. "You are excellent at ___, and I think you can go even further if you master _____."

Someone Asks You Questions That You
Already Answered in an Email

Situation	You send someone emails with specific information. They don't seem to read them and ask you questions about what you've already spent 20 minutes writing.
Script	*Can you help me with something? I've noticed that when I put information in emails, you don't seem to respond. I'm not sure if you're getting them or if we communicate differently. What's the best way to ensure that we are on the same page?*

Component	Phrase
Asking for help	*Can you help me with something?*
Clarification request	*I'm not sure if you're getting them or if we communicate differently.*

Rationale	People communicate differently. The real problem that you're trying to solve isn't about email; it's about how to make sure they have the important information without you wasting your time. Opening up this conversation will save time for both of you.

Someone Sends Ultra-Long Emails

Situation	Someone sends you extra-long emails that suck up your time and energy.
Script	*Could you do me a favor? Could you please do three short bullet points at the top of your email to tell me what to attend to? I am often short on time, and this approach will ensure that I can address the items that are most important to you.*

Component	Phrase
Asking for help	*Could you do me a favor?*
Need statement	*Could you please do three short bullet points at the top of your email to tell me what to attend to? I am often short on time...*
Affirmation	*I can address the items that are most important to you.*
Rationale	Asking for a favor automatically engages the other person's desire to help. Because they are thinking about how to help you, they are less likely to get defensive when you offer a suggestion. Stating your specific preference and combining it with the desire to address their needs helps them understand that their opinion is valued. They will be more likely to change their behavior to ensure that it is heard.

Someone Is Trying to Involve You in "People Drama"

Situation	A colleague sends you an email saying that a coworker is distant and cold. It is clear that he wants some type of response from you. You want to be viewed as supportive, but you don't want to be involved in drama.
Script	*That sounds rough. I hope it works out.* or *I'm sorry. I hope it works out.*

Component	Phrase
Their feelings, downgraded	*That sounds rough.*
Social apology	*I'm sorry.*

Rationale	You want to be kind but noncommittal in your response. If you reference the specific situation, your words could be misinterpreted and instantly pull you into the conflict.
Alternative Action	It's fine not to respond. If the person checks in later, you can simply say that you didn't have a response / any thoughts.

You Feel Pressure to Engage in Late Drinks on a Business Trip

Situation	You are on a business trip and are meeting with people who could benefit your business. Everyone wants to go out for drinks, but you have a lot of pressing work to do (or you just don't want to participate).
Script	*I'd love to meet up with all of you, but I also have some pressing business to address. I'm going to stop by for an hour or two and then I may leave early. (Alternately, you can stop by later— figure out the time frame that will have maximum benefit.)*

Component	Phrase
No-yes	*I also have some pressing business to address. I'm going to stop by for an hour or two.*
Affirmation	*I'd love to meet up with all of you.*

Rationale	**Disclaimer 1:** In each situation, you need to gauge the stakes, atmosphere, and social equity that may transpire. Further, pay attention to the dynamics and where great conversation is most likely to happen. Apart from that, showing up for part of the time is often a great compromise. Familiarity is a social psychology principle in which we automatically trust people who are familiar to us. (This is why repetitive advertising works, by the way.) People usually won't judge you for coming later or leaving early; what they'll remember is that you were there. **Disclaimer 2:** If there is a lot of pressure and you feel that you *will* be judged, you may want to be aware that this is a pink flag in terms of whether those involved will be good partners, vendors, etc. Great business and personal relationships are based on boundaries and respect—of time, money, and other priorities.

An Acquaintance Wants You to Use Her Services

Situation	Someone in your network approaches you and offers services that seem appropriate for you / your business. You are unsure if it is the right fit for you.
Script	*Thank you for letting me know about your services. Right now, I'm just trying to assess the best fit as I grow my business. I'll definitely keep you in mind as an option. (If the person pushes, add "I don't want to make promises until I know I can commit.)*

Component	**Phrase**
Affirmation	*Thank you for letting me know about your services.*
Pause creation	*Right now, I'm just trying to assess the best fit as I grow my business.*
No-yes	*I'm just trying to assess the best fit...I'll definitely keep you in mind.*
Alternate Script	If you know it's not the right fit and the person is pushing the issue, it will save you both time and emotion to say, "Thank you so much for the offer. I just don't think that it's going to be the right fit for us. I would feel bad moving forward and then having it not work out." It's still soft, but you close the door.
Rationale	Great business relationships are built on fit and mutual respect. If you make promises to avoid hurting someone's feelings in the moment, you may agree to something that is not the right fit for you. If you do that, the transaction won't work long-term and you will eventually hurt their feelings anyway.

SOCIAL

Someone Asks You a Personal Question—
You Don't Want to Answer

Situation	Someone with whom you have regular contact asks you about your sex life, your childhood, why you don't have children, your health history, political view, religious view...you get the picture.
Script	*I'm not comfortable discussing that right now. Maybe we'll talk about it in the future sometime. So, did you do anything fun this weekend?* or *It's a long, boring answer. Maybe we'll get to it sometime.*

Component	Phrase
"No" statement	*I'm not comfortable discussing that.*
No-yes	*Maybe we'll talk about it in the future sometime.*
Distraction	*So, did you do anything fun this weekend?*

Rationale	The "no" statement says that you are not going to answer the question. The reason that you keep the door slightly open to a future discussion is because it reduces the perception of scarcity. Everyone wants what they can't have. If you give a solid "no," the person becomes more curious and more intent on getting an answer. Acting as if it's not a big deal and that you might tell them at some point lessens the mystery and their need to get answers. Asking about the weekend additionally diverts focus from your life onto theirs and provides a way for the conversation to continue to flow.

Exception	If a stranger or passing acquaintance asks you, it's fine to say, "I'm not comfortable discussing that." You can always add humor. "I could tell you, but then I'd have to kill you." "I need money to have that type of discussion." "It's a long, boring answer."
Follow-Up Actions	If a person persists, say, "I'm curious, why is this so important to you?" Rationale—you've just flipped the script and put him or her on the spot. Additionally, maybe there is information in his answer that allows you to answer the part of the question that is important to him but not the parts that are personal to you.

Social Pressure

Situation	You are at a social gathering, and you want to leave early. One or several people beg you to stay "just another 30 minutes."
Script	*You are all fabulous, but I promised myself an early night.* or *I do need to go, but I would love to stay longer if I could.*

Component	**Phrase**
Affirmation	*You are all fabulous; I would love to stay longer if I could.*
Need statement	*I promised myself an early night; I do need to go.*
Rationale	State the basics and include the affirmation. The action is the key step. If people believe that social pressure will get you to cave, they will continue to try until there is some type of signal that it's not going to happen.
Action	Collect your keys and begin walking toward the door.
Tricia-Style Script Option	(Laughing) "You know who is going to win this, right?" "Tricia-style" is an overt egotistical statement that comes with a wink. "You know who is going to win, right?" It comes from a deep-seated confidence in my boundaries that allows me to be almost arrogant but in a playful way. If you lack personal confidence or playfulness, stay with the basics or you'll just come across as a jerk.

You Want to Decline a Social Event Because You Are Tired

© Dr. Tricia Groff

Situation	You are invited to a social event. You don't have a competing obligation, but you want to take the time to refuel.
Script	*I'm sorry; I can't make it.* or *I'm struggling to catch up, and I need some downtime. Otherwise, I'd love to join you.*

Component	Phrase
Social apology	*I'm sorry.*
"No" statement	*I can't make it.*
Need statement	*I need some downtime.*
Affirmation	*Otherwise, I'd love to join you.*

Rationale	The phrase you use depends on your comfort and familiarity with the group. The first statement gives no explanation ("no" statement). The second gives an explanation and affirms the group's importance to you. If you use the second explanation, make a point to attend the next gathering to substantiate your comment that "you'd love to join" ("no" statement, affirmation).
Long-Term Sanity	Over time, you want to build relationships only with people who support your well-being. These people will not take it personally when you opt out. If you have family members who are pressuring you, alternate saying yes and no until you train them that you may or may not attend all functions.

You Need to Turn Someone Down after the Third Date

Situation	You've seen someone romantically a few times, but you've decided that you don't want to move further into a relationship.
Script	*I've been thinking, and I don't think this is going to be a good fit for me. I wanted to let you know so as not to waste your time.*

Component	Phrase
Statement of position	*I don't think this is going to be a good fit for me.*
Acknowledgment of other's needs	*So as not to waste your time*

Rationale	People want the bottom line, fast. Dragging out the bottom line simply makes it excruciating for both of you.
Follow-Up Script: If the Other Person Says "Why?"	**Script:** There's not a specific reason; I just don't feel the (fit, chemistry, etc.) that I'm looking for in a relationship. **Rationale on Follow-Up:** There are two reasons for the vague answer to the "why?" First, if it's a good person, why create unnecessary wounds by listing flaws that may be perfectly acceptable to someone else? Second, if there are raging red character flags, you don't want to give information that would help the person lie / mask them for the next person. **Exception:** Notice that there is a three-date notation on this situation. If you are ending a long-term relationship, extra discussion and information may be helpful for closure.

SPOUSES, FRIENDS, AND OTHER CLOSE RELATIONSHIPS

Hurt Feelings (Your Partner's)

Situation	You were focused on work and forgot something important.
Script	*I'm sorry. I didn't mean to make you feel second place or less special.*

Component	Phrase
Acknowledgment of potential wrongdoing	*I'm sorry.*
Acknowledgment of other's feelings	*I didn't mean to make you feel second place or less special.*
Rationale	The anatomy of hurt feelings is that someone does something that makes us feel less important to them than we thought we were.
Follow-Up Actions	First, do something to show them you are sorry, preferably in the way that they will be most likely to understand. Some people will be moved by a small gift, others by extra quality time (see *The 5 Love Languages* by Gary Chapman). Second, figure out a plan to correct the problem. If you aren't sure that your plan works, ask their opinion.

You and Your Spouse Have a Circular Argument That Needs a Solution

Situation	You think that you should hire someone to help clean the house or help with the children. Your spouse disagrees. You argue about the problem on a regular basis.
Script	*Honey, I know we've been going round and round about this. Could we set a time to think of creative options and a game plan that would be okay for both of us? I'm worried that if we don't, I'll keep getting frustrated/being a jerk, and I don't want to do that with you.*

Component	Phrase
Affirmation	*Honey, I don't want to do that with you.*
Your feelings	*I'm worried.*
Rationale	In any relationship worth keeping, you want to highlight the importance of the relationship rather than the importance of winning the argument at hand. (Winning and toasting alone is a pyrrhic victory.)

You Need to Give Tough-Love Feedback
to Someone You Care About

Situation	A client, family member, or friend trusts you enough to be honest if you notice something that is not working. You see him or her doing something that doesn't fit in the success equation.
Script	*I have to say something. This is going to hurt.* (Deliver a "straight-to-the-point" message.) or *I need to say something and I'm not sure exactly how. I'm worried about hurting your feelings.*

Component	Phrase
Heads-up	*This is going to hurt.*
Need statement	*I have to say something.*
Request for help (subtle)	*I'm not sure exactly how*
Your feelings	*I'm worried.*
Acknowledgment of their feelings	*About hurting your feelings*

Rationale	**Script 1:** Saying, "This is going to hurt," gives people a second to brace themselves. Additionally, because you call it out immediately, they can intuit that your intention is not to hurt them. **Script 2:** Saying what is in your head instantly allows the other person to know what is going on. Invariably, they try to help you. "It's okay; just say it."
Tricia-Style Script Option	**Following the Feedback:** "Just to let you know, there aren't many people that have enough balls to even have this conversation. Also, I'll tell you the tough stuff, but that also means that when I give you compliments, I'm not just blowing smoke."

Ignorant Ass

Situation	It's the person at dinner who is a total bigot and totally proud of it. He or she says _____ group can't be trusted.
Script	*I have friends in that group. I think they're okay.* or *Everyone has an opinion.*

Component	Phrase
Mild statement of position	*I think they're okay.*
Noncommittal show of position	*Everyone has an opinion.*

Rationale	Unless you are bored out of your mind, there is no reason to engage in an intellectual argument with someone who is ignorantly proud of being a bigot. The first option allows you to "say something" if you feel ethically bound to acknowledge your disagreement. The second option is a total opt-out.
Follow-Up Action If the Ignorant Ass Persists with the Conversation	**Script:** Let's agree to disagree. So tell me about the new car/job/house. **Rationale:** The ignorant ass will like to talk about himself or herself. It will still be annoying, but at least you can divert the conversation to less sensitive topics.

Food Pusher

Situation	Aunt Martha makes the best brownies ever, and to her, food is love. You are following a low-carb plan.
Script	*I'm not hungry for any right now, but they look fantastic.*

Component	Phrase
"No" statement	*I'm not hungry for any right now.*
Affirmation	*They look fantastic.*

Rationale	Admitting a diet to a food pusher is like waving a red flag to a bull. The best way is to avoid the conversation. The addition of the words "right now" appeases people faster than a hard "no."
Follow-Up Action	If Aunt Martha keeps pushing, ask if you can take some to go. Take two and give them to your neighbor or fertilize the garbage can.

KEY TAKEAWAYS

1. *Remember that you can create a pause if you are not sure what to say in the moment.*

2. *When you use one of these scripts or create one of your own, make a little mental note of the outcome. Over time, it will be easier for you to figure out what to say in the moment, in a way that feels right to you.*

YOU'VE GOT THIS

One fine Sunday, in the middle of editing this book, I looked at what I had written on anger. I ensured that "never write an email when you are angry" had the appropriate capitalization to drive the point home. It said, *NEVER, EVER* write an email when you are angry. Late that night, I witnessed what I perceived as racial targeting toward a professional who was trying to help me. Sickened to my stomach and needing to take action before I went to sleep, I sent a blunt, angry email to a powerful contact. I forgot that my contact forwards emails without permission, and phone lines were lighting up by the next morning. Oops.

In my defense, a little rage on social injustice is a good thing. At the same time, I violated what I had just written about anger, holding your cards close, and waiting until emotion recedes. Epic fail. I returned to the manuscript. Feeling like a hypocrite for violating what I had adamantly emphasized, I took the all-caps out of the sentence.

Remember, at the beginning of the book, when I told you that you will always be in the learning curve about yourself and others? It's true for you and for me too. We will not get everything right. As we live, we continually encounter new situations for which we do not have a response template. Part of increasing your confidence in your soft skills means understanding that no one gets it right all the time. When you make a mistake, you're not a failure. When you veer off course, assess the antecedents and figure out what you can do differently the next time.

As I wrote this book, new questions and situations continued to arise. I wanted to keep adding to the book, but I'm not sure that a 600-page book is a good idea. As a compromise, I've set up the *www.relationalgenius.com* website where you can go for additional information and resources.

What's next? You're a high achiever, so you're going to try to implement everything at once. Don't do that. Pick one tactic that seems effortless and one that feels a little scary. Implement both. Assess the outcomes. Revise as needed. Then add the next one.

Remember that people are who they are, not who you want them to be. That goes for you too. Give yourself grace when you don't measure up to your standards. Remember that you are not alone. You are amazing. You are lovable, and you are loved. You have a special gift to give to this world. You're a relational genius. You've got this.

SPECIAL THANKS

COVID-19 hit the United States two days after I sent my rough draft to a few trusted people. In the midst of that initial chaos, Penny Cowden, president of Philanthropy 212, took the time to read and provide feedback on the book. Penny lives and breathes the values of philanthropy, but her faith and enduring support during a difficult year is the embodiment of generosity. (Find Penny at *www.philanthropy212.com*.)

Kathy Jo Stence, also immersed in managing life and family amid COVID, painstakingly read all of the pages, in all of their very rough-draft glory. Kathy Jo, you are a rare and beautiful treasure, and I am lucky to have you as a friend.

Thank you, Carolyn Weaver, for your ongoing friendship and support through the years. Thank you for helping me with read-ability and for overnighting a pink mask so that I could stylishly protect my clients.

Janae Cardel, your unflagging support and genuine interest means more than you will ever know. Thank you for listening to the tedious updates and for reminding me of my "why" when I got tired.

Lauren Nelson, I adore you—you add pink and purple sparkles to my existence. Thank you for listening to me spin about the title and cover. More than anything, thank you for October 2019, when you said, "Tricia, just write the book." I feel safe with you, and I can't think of a bigger compliment.

Nicole Wayde, I never have to make myself smaller around you, and you are never surprised by my successes. Thank you for your input on Dr. Tirado's tie, for the shared margaritas, and for doing life with me.

Al Forsyth, I didn't reference research, and I didn't use statistics. I did, however, reach into my passion for helping people, a value that you have modeled since day one. I hope you like this. The truth is, I would never have written it if I hadn't met you. Thank you for believing in me.

Polly, my friend and graphic designer at Polly Graphic Design, thank you for your expertise, your compassion, and your patience. Thank you for helping me to build a brand that allows me to live in color. (Polly is a goddess; find her at *www.pollygraphic.com*.)

Terry Zechman, I'm not sure that I will ever be able to explain what happened on the day you took the headshot for this book. What I do know is that when people see me at my most vulnerable and have my back (and my hair), they have my loyalty forever.

Greg Houston, I've always imagined thought bubbles to reflect the disparity between what people show and what they are actually thinking. I am so excited that I found you. Thank you for your easy style, for your fast communication, and for your skill in bringing visual interest to this book. (Find Greg at *www.fiverr.com/ quickcartoon*.)

Scribe Media. Thank you, Natalie, for the orchestration of the process and the bonus creativity you brought for navigating stuck points. Miles, the day I met you was a highlight of this process. Thank you for "getting it." Thank you, John, for your thoughtful and detailed feedback. Ronnie, the way you helped me turn a client nickname into a title still makes me laugh. Thank you.

My daddy—who is hanging out with Jesus. Thank you for loving me and accepting me when I chose to walk my own path. I don't know if you would have read this book, but you still would have been proud of me for writing it.

First and last, my clients. When I was in my twenties, the adults around me laughed at the idea of making money while doing something I loved. I've learned that doing something I love with people I respect is everything. Thank you for trusting me to be part of your life. And thank you for answering the weird poll questions I asked as I wrote this.

ABOUT THE AUTHOR

Dr. Tricia Groff is a board-licensed psychologist and executive coach who specializes in high achievers. She integrates her love of technology, innovation, business, and leadership by coaching CEO founders and their organizations.

Dr. Groff obtained her PhD, master's, and bachelor's in psychology, winning honors and awards at each level of her education. With over 20 years of experience, she focuses on strategies for leadership excellence, personal fulfillment, and professional satisfaction. She also applies psychology to enhance workplace culture, decision-making, and team cohesion during company growth.

In a world that pressures people to maintain the status quo, Dr. Groff prefers to challenge it. She believes that integrity can coexist with success; kindness can coexist with competition; intellect can coexist with emotion; and business profit can coexist with great work cultures. Her life passion revolves around calling out the greatness in those around her and letting them know that they are loved.

Dr. Groff works and plays in sunny Arizona. Following her work hard / play hard approach to life balance, she hates people before 9 a.m., loves driving fast, and refuses to choose between success and happiness.

For more information about Dr. Groff's services, visit *www. drtriciagroff.com.* For additional resources, visit *www.relational genius.com.*